JANE AUSTEN

BY

R. BRIMLEY JOHNSON

HASKELL HOUSE PUBLISHERS Ltd.

Publishers of Scarce Scholarly Books

NEW YORK, N. Y. 10012

1974

HASKELL HOUSE PUBLISHERS Ltd.

Publishers of Scarce Scholarly Books

280 LAFAYETTE STREET

NEW YORK, N. Y. 10012

Library of Congress Cataloging in Publication Data

Johnson, Reginald Brimley, 1867-1932.
  Jane Austen.

  Reprint of the 1927 ed.
  1. Austen, Jane, 1775-1817.
PR4036.J6 1974   823'.7 [B]   74-1102
ISBN 0-8383-1746-4

Printed in the United States of America

CONTENTS

JANE AUSTEN

CHAPTER I

MANNERS

*Mr Darcy "is a gentleman ; I am a gentleman's daughter :
so far we are equal," said Elizabeth.—"Emma spoke on
being entreated. What did she say ? Just what she ought,
of course. A lady always does."* Such is the drastic
finality that characterises every utterance of Jane
Austen's upon propriety.

For the Austens, we must remember, belong to the
period and the class which was dominated by the County ;
and the County, unlike "the professions," did not think,
they knew. The author of *Pride and Prejudice* always
identified herself on social questions with her "class," as
intelligently represented by her family : and in these
matters I am convinced that she never made a mistake.

The vicarage was not itself quite the County ; but
though distinctions were more clear and rigid in those
days than in ours, there was also more conventional
mingling on terms of acknowledged equality. Elizabeth,
you will observe, only declared that "we are equal *so far.*"
She did not ignore the difference. Darcy was "County" ;

so were Knightley and the Musgroves in a small way; the Bennets, the Woodhouses, and the Austens were not. Elizabeth obviously enjoyed a nice comfortable noisy game of lottery-tickets, and a little bit of hot supper to follow.

It is difficult for us, sometimes, to accept the complacent assumptions of the novels, and Jane Austen's *Letters*, without regarding the writer, for all her charm, as a snob. Scott, indeed, said that her heroines, if not mercenary, always selected husbands a little "above" themselves, pursuing eligibles with good taste.

There are four questions, and four only, on which Jane Austen ever expressed her own private opinions: one moral standard for the sexes, the education of girls, "those places in town for the sale, not quite of human flesh, but of human intellect," and the privelige claimed for women "of loving longest, when existence or when hope is gone."

But Emma Woodhouse once "forgot" herself towards Miss Bates; Miss Bingley always forgot that her money had been acquired in trade; Mr Collins "found out, by a singular accident," that he was—actually—in the same room with "a near relation of his patroness." We know what Jane Austen thought of snobs.

It has been whispered that Darcy himself was not a perfect gentleman; but the criticism ignores his cheerful courtesy to the estimable Gardiners who lived in Grace-church Street, though they did "keep a manservant." Elizabeth could only suppose that partiality for their niece had blinded him to their connections in the city; but Jane Austen knew better. Under any circumstances, Mr Gardiner would have been quite at home; where Uncle Philips, "breathing port wine," could never enter, and Sir William Lucas could only bow in grateful silence.

There are several memorable occasions, again, on which her great folk stand revealed as very perfect knights. Sir Thomas Bertram not only refrained from pressing the claims of Crawford upon the "fearful" Fanny, but saw to it that a comfortable fire was lighted in her room; Mr Knightley once asked Harriet to dance; Darcy was courteous to Lydia, under most trying circumstances; and Henry Crawford treated Susan, Mrs Price, and her husband with almost astonishing respect. Equal insight taught the novelist to show us how General Tilney and Sir Walter Elliot disgraced their breeding from purely personal faults of character and disposition.

Catherine Morland and Fanny, on the other hand, were a little below the Austens; though all her other heroines were absolutely one of themselves: their precise position perhaps most clearly revealed in the Dashwoods because, like them, Jane Austen lived, at least in the latter years, in a similar peculiar, but intimate, relation between the cottage and the Great House, on her brother Edward (Knight's) estate: a delightful and widening experience, elsewhere spoiled by personal, inherited, vulgarity in the case of Mary Musgrove.

We must finally remark that young ladies like the Austens could "move up" into the County by marriage, without derision from their new relatives or embarrassment to themselves. "Among the merits and the happiness of Elinor and Marianne, let it not be reckoned as the least considerable, that though sisters, and living almost within sight of each other, they could live without disagreement between themselves, or producing coolness between their husbands" : yet Brandon was Edward's patron.

It must be noted further, to our confusion, that where no doubt could ever exist as to who was, or was not, within the pale, greater variety of breeding or manners was permitted the individual. Convention must always allow more personal liberty, than reason or private judgment. The test is not, what are you; but who are you. Darcy defied his aunt, but would never have acknowledged her not quite a lady ; and Elizabeth gave offence because she dared to judge even the elect more by character than by caste. No one cut the Palmers or Mrs Jennings.

On the other hand, Knightley valued Robert Martin no less than Larkins and appreciated his conversation; but, to please Emma, he would "alter his rank in society if he could." "As a composition" Robert's letter to Harriet "would not have disgraced a gentleman. . . . It expressed good sense, warm attachment, liberality, propriety, even delicacy of feeling. . . . I understand the sort of mind. Vigorous, decided, with sentiments to a certain point not coarse." Yet "I had no idea he could be so very clownish, so totally without air. I had

imagined him, I confess, a degree or two nearer gentility."

In fact "the yeomanry are precisely the order of people
with whom I feel I can have nothing to do. A degree or
two lower, and a credible appearance might interest me;
I might hope to be useful to their families in some way
or other. But a farmer can need none of my help, and is,
therefore, in one sense, as much above my notice, as in
every other way he is below it."

There were reasons, of course, for Emma's outspoken
disparagement of Robert Martin; but Knightley himself
would place him, with equal assurance, below even that
"come-at-able second set . . . of low origin, and only
moderately genteel," the Perrys, and the Coles. Lucy
Steele was an upstart.

It is a nice distinction, no doubt; which should serve
to remind us, nevertheless, how hard it was—and indeed
remains—to distinguish the various pretensions which
have defined the great English middle-class, whether of
the upper, lower, or middle kind.

For Jane Austen, and the persons of her fiction, were
indubitably middle-class; that new-born variety of the
genus homo, which in the previous century embraced, I
think, Lord Chesterfield and Dr Johnson, Sir Charles
Grandison and Tom Jones. In some fashion they were
all gentlefolk.

The special difficulty for modern readers, of recognising
the breed, is no doubt chiefly due to the conspicuous
absence of the professions; and the almost complete

indifference to London "sets." The clergy alone, to be considered later; and the Navy, for purely personal reasons, are here permitted to meet the squire; and it is this lack of intellectual influences which explains Miss Austen's apparently conventional outlook on life, her willingness to adopt the verdicts of her class; as they had mainly inherited them from an earlier, more exclusive, nobility; and were by such means, at that time, creating and maintaining the national type—not yet tempted to question authority or discuss an established faith. They were both serious and sincere; only governed by tradition, not by thought. *Individual* persons and deeds were subject to private judgment: ethics and manners determined by rule.

I suspect, however, that the Austens in real life were in certain ways a little more independent of convention, and certainly more content with themselves, than the majority of Jane's fiction persons: in part, no doubt, because two influences—then as now—secured their personal gentility: the University and the Church. Mr Collins, we know, "belonged to one of the universities," but he "had merely kept the necessary terms, without forming at it any useful acquaintance." Jane's great-uncle Theophilus Leigh, however, was essentially a university man, the true "don" type; and her father, the "handsome proctor," was indubitably academic. As his children were mainly educated at home, his influence no doubt gave them comparatively broad minds and cultured judgment; a little independent, and in advance, of the County code. The clergy, too, were no longer held down to the position of superior family servants; but could, even if underbred like Mr Elton, aspire to a Miss Woodhouse. He is the only "gentleman," I think, Jane Austen ever observed "in drink"; and, if his condition offended the lady, it does not appear to have degraded "the cloth." Tilney, Edmund, and the unfortunate Edward Ferrars, were all typical younger sons—in effect, if not in fact.

The clergy, perhaps, may be said to have occupied a position somewhat similar to that of the second or third son in good families. Given sufficient personality and a decent education, they could sit above the salt ; accepted, and generally welcome, to men of a, technically, higher position in the world and probably of far greater wealth. We are surprised, perhaps, by their likeness to others, and one scarcely isolates them at all. The County did not share Miss Crawford's objections to Edmund Bertram, though possibly a layman might have been less critical of her. The vicar looked after his parish, but remained a man of the world: largely immune fortunately from the fluttering attentions of feminine imbecility—the terror of generations to come, when Eltons were more in vogue.

Wherefore everything combined to fix superiority upon the Austens—a social assurance which, being theirs without effort, never tempted to arrogance or self-assertion, unless wantonly provoked by a Lady Catherine or a Miss Bingley.

There is, however, one aspect of this contented and established gentility, which remains somewhat baffling, if not distasteful, to modern minds. How did they occupy themselves or exercise their intelligence? Did they spend their days, like Lady Bertram, "in sitting nicely dressed on a sofa, doing some long piece of needlework, of little use and no beauty ? "

To us their existence appears a chronicle of most incredibly small beer. Some, indeed, condemn the novels, or cannot read them, on this account. There is a hint of such criticism, or comment on life, in Emma's friendship with Harriet Smith. The persistent folly of that intimacy would never have been provoked, had Miss Woodhouse possessed a taste for any serious or sensible occupation : had she played and sung as well as Jane Fairfax, or loved books like Marianne Dashwood. Yet, after all, I suspect Miss Austen only intended to draw an *im*perfect heroine; without a thought of reflecting upon the emptiness of life. The Misses Bertram were "bored" by their own folly; while Elizabeth and Anne Elliot never appear at a loss for occupation, though not abnormally accomplished or absorbed by enthusiasm.

"It is amazing to me," said Bingley, "how young ladies can have patience to be so very accomplished as they all are. They all paint tables, cover screens, and net purses." Eliza Bennet, being "one of those young ladies who seek to recommend themselves to the other sex by undervaluing their own," frankly derided the young man's modest "list of accomplishments"; but the point of interest to us remains,—that he regarded such strenuous occupations as evidence of a superior mind, one somewhat above the ordinary pleasures of life.

The ladies of that generation were not a great deal occupied about the house, though they did beautiful needlework; dress was not sufficiently complicated to demand long hours of blissful concentration, and only the foolish Lydias enjoyed shopping for its own sake. Maybe they "read all such works as heroines must read to supply their memories with those quotations which are so serviceable and so soothing in the vicissitudes of their eventful lives." Here Emma no doubt was guided with discretion by "poor Miss Taylor," as Edmund "recommended the books which charmed Fanny's leisure hours, encouraged her taste, and corrected her judgment." On the other hand, Benwick was *mis*directed by "a broken heart"; Isabella devoured everything "shocking that came out"; as Mary Bennet was plain, she "read great books and made extracts." Only Henry and Miss Tilney, Anne Elliot and Mr Crawford were really cultured; though Marianne had good taste from genuine enthusiasm, and Darcy was "always buying books for a library that had been the work of many generations."

Yet the social position of Robert Martin was most clearly defined by his lack of "information beyond the line of his own business. He does not read . . . just as it should be. What has he to do with books?"

Miss Austen, clearly, expected young people to read; therein providing the only sensible occupation—as it would seem to us—for their long hours of leisure. Of her own special interest in books, I shall say more in its proper place.

There was, however, a great deal of "neighbourliness" among friends. The "call"—at such congenial homes as Randalls or on such cheerful companions as the Crawfords, was not made from a sense of duty. It was not only silly girls like Catherine and Isabella who parted affectionately in the morning, happy in "learning, to their mutual relief, that they should see each other across the theatre at night, and say their prayers in the same chapel the next morning." Anne, indeed, "had always thought such a style of intercourse highly imprudent"; but it was the "continual subjects of offence" due to her sister's jealousy, not the habit itself, which she deplored. The merely formal "call" Miss Austen dismissed with more drastic severity:—"They came, and they sat, and they went."

On the other hand, she knew the gain, which might also contain a moral lesson, of visiting one's relations. She had not needed "this visit to Uppercross to learn that a removal from one set of people to another, though at a distance of only three miles, will often include a total change of conversation, opinion and idea"; a change, of course, which Jane Austen's letters reveal as both stimulating and delightful: apart from her special appreciation of its humorous opportunities.

There were somewhat frequent "parties," more or less formal, to occupy winter evenings pleasantly: for Jane Austen would never have accepted John Knightley's ungracious attack upon "the folly of not allowing people to be comfortable at home, and the folly of people's not staying comfortably at home when they can! . . . Going in dismal weather, to return probably in worse;—four horses and four servants taken out for nothing but to convey five, idle, shivering creatures into colder rooms and worse company than they might have at home."

Her view of the matter was kindlier and more cheerful:— "We do not want for amusement: bilbocatch, at which George is indefatigable, spillikins, paper ships, riddles, conundrums and cards, with watching the flow and ebb of the river, and now and then a stroll out, keep us well employed." Mr Austen-Leigh declared that "none of them could throw spillikins in so perfect a circle, or take them off with so steady a hand," as Jane. "Her performances with the cup-and-ball were marvellous. She has been known to catch the ball on the point above a hundred times in succession." Mr Collins was always ready to lose "five shillings" at "a card table"; as "thanks to Lady Catherine de Burgh, he was removed far beyond the necessity of regarding little matters"; though I am afraid he might have shared Knightley's "alarm and indignation" at Frank Churchill's "deeper game" with his young nephew's "alphabets."

Summer, again, brought with it the varied pleasures of "exploring . . . in a large bonnet and one of my little baskets hanging on my arm . . . a table spread in the shade, you know."

But, after all, the chief resource of those days was the dance—private or public, often entirely informal.

"It may be possible to do without dancing entirely. Instances have been known of young people passing many, many months successively without being at any ball of any description, and no material injury accrue either to body or mind; but when a beginning is made —when the felicities of rapid motion have once been, though slightly, felt—it must be a heavy set that does not ask for more."

A hundred gay passages in the *Letters* reveal the fact that Jane's own "set" was no heavier than her heroine's. "I fancy I could just as well dance for a week together as for half an hour . . . it was the same room in which we danced fifteen years ago. I thought it all over, and in spite of the shame of being so much older, felt with thankfulness that I was quite as happy now as then." I have no belief in her pretended content to "leave off being young," or that she ever found "many *douceurs* in being a sort of *chaperon*," though she *was* "put on the sofa near the fire, and could drink as much wine as she liked."

She had not, in reality, passed on far from the pretty *ingénue's* emotions after her first ball; for Fanny Price, too, there was "one moment and no more, to view the happy scene and take a last look at the five or six determined couples who were still hard at work—and then,

creeping slowly up the principal staircase, pursued by
the ceaseless country-dance, feverish with hopes and
fears, soup and negus, sore-footed and fatigued, restless
and agitated, yet feeling, in spite of everything, that a
ball was indeed delightful."

There were, of course, more frequent gaieties at Bath,
"with its balls or concerts on each alternate evening";
its "Sunday crowd of fashionables," and "the splendid
barouche, dashing curricle, elegant tandem, and gentlemen on horseback." The only town, we are told by its
historian, "where young women indiscriminately run
either alone or in groups from one end to the other without any servant or steady friend to accompany them,
talking and laughing at the corners of the streets, and
walking sometimes with young men only!"

Southampton, again, we are surprised to learn from
Miss Mitford, "in the total absence of the vulgar hurry
of business or the chilling apathy of fashion, was, indeed,
all life, all gaiety, and had an airiness, an animation
which might become the capital of fairyland." The
Assembly Rooms "were very elegantly fitted up." We
share Tennyson's indignation at Lyme Regis:—"Don't
talk to me of the Duke of Monmouth. Show me the
exact spot where Louisa Musgrove fell."

One other diversion, an indispensable feature of
domestic fiction, I am convinced, was then cultivated
to a fine art—the "nice" flirtation. No one, we admit,
has been more severe than Jane Austen upon the vulgar
adepts—Lydia Bennet, the Thorpes, and Captain Tilney.

But Emma and Elizabeth were able practitioners; Frank Churchill and the Henrys (Crawford and Tilney) were past-masters of the craft; even Marianne's unblushing partiality for "dearest Willoughby," though unconsciously selfish and inconsiderate, never exceeded the limits of good taste or was condemned by the Code.

We do not flirt to-day so elegantly as the Victorians. There is little occasion; now that a boy and girl may be long inseparable, without anyone asking their "intentions"; and intimacy may, in fact, be indulged without self-consciousness of sex.

On the other hand, though our grandparents' flirtations had no connection whatever with the passion-episodes or complexes of modern fiction, they did involve conduct and conversation deliberately provocative of what makes life worth living, the mysterious affinities, born of difference, between the sexes: a modestly arch attitude towards the chosen friend, which brought out character and charm.

I have elsewhere noted that, under Victorian conventions, men and women had no other means of coming to know each other before marriage, no other chance of wisely selecting a mate. In studying the delightful freedom of our own younger set, I have often recalled an older woman's mature condemnation of her girlhood's stupid and priggish aversion to those who were what she then called "horrid about men"; but whom from a broader outlook, she could now applaud for their wise and agreeable courage.

Jane Austen has given this art to her favourite
heroines; and though quizzing herself and her own
efficiency, I believe that a chance word in her private
letters actually reveals a significant truth:—"Mr H.
began with Elizabeth, and afterwards danced with her
again; but *they* do not know how *to be particular*. I
flatter myself, however, that they will profit by the
three successive lessons which I have given them."
Elsewhere she pities "three elder sisters, *who had so
little of that kind of youth*," and prefers "little, smiling,
flirting Julia" to a more sedate "Miss."

We do not, of course, accept Miss Mitford's second-
hand reminiscence of "the prettiest, silliest, most
affected, husband-hunting butterfly"; but we note that
her widow cousin, Eliza, Comtesse de Feuillade, afterwards Mrs Henry Austen, was "not unwilling to change
her estate again, but loth to give up (as she said) "dear
liberty and dearer flirtation." And Jane loved Eliza.

Hers was, above all, an eagerly sociable nature; and
it was her love for gay, simple-minded, even frivolous,
young people that gave supreme virtue to her art.

CHAPTER II

MORALS

"*Since the ——shire were first quartered in Meryton,*" *said* *Elizabeth,* "*nothing but love, flirtation and officers have been in Lydia's head.   She has been doing everything in her power by thinking and talking on the subject, to give greater —what shall I call it ?—susceptibility to her feelings, which are naturally lively enough . . . the elopement had been brought on by the strength of her love rather than by his ; . . . his flight was rendered necessary by distress of circumstances ; and . . . he was not the young man to resist an opportunity of having a companion.*"

To Wickham, in fact, the adventure had been no more than an agreeable episode: "he still cherished the hope of more effectually making his fortune by marriage in some other country," as he had once attempted it with Miss Darcy and on another occasion with "ten thousand pounds" and Miss King.

Lydia, too, had not until the last moment exhibited "any partiality for him" . . . though never reticent about her affairs, "she had wanted only encouragement to attach herself to any body." Anticipating the joys of Brighton she "saw herself seated beneath a tent, tenderly flirting with at least six officers at once."

It was in fact her "susceptibility," which to-day would be called passion, that determined her conduct and satisfied her feelings.

Writing later of Maria Bertram, Mrs Rushworth, Jane Austen is not afraid of the word. Her "passions," indeed, were "strong" and concentrated upon a particular object—the far more fascinating Henry Crawford. She had been cold to him from "anger on Fanny's account," thus awakening his vanity "to subdue so proud a display of resentment": and when secure of his "attentions," revealed her love.

It is true that the *word* passion is not used here with its precise significance, since Henry, we read, had loved Fanny "rationally as well as passionately," and even Edmund required time to "cure his unconquerable passion" for Mary. In this respect, Lydia stands alone.

But these "unfortunate affairs" surely disclose the fact that Miss Austen was neither ignorant nor blind on subjects of which she seldom cared to write; though Colonel Brandon and Mrs Clay give further occasion to prove she did not shirk them.

It is rather her clean-cut, almost cool, definition of sin, and her unhesitating punishments, that offend certain modern readers: still more, perhaps, the uncomfortable suspicion that Elizabeth was, in her heart, more alarmed by the probable "consequences" for herself than by "doubt of a sister's sense of decency and virtue."

The "nice" people in the novels seem a little hard on vulgarity and folly; the virtuous rather uncharitable

towards vice—save when Elinor weakens towards
Willoughby.

One explanation will be discussed later; but her reticence and her judgments were both in accord with the
conventions of her own people; and were also due to her
obvious distaste for moralising in fiction. Every word
here, with one remarkable exception, is directed to particular cases. It is not that Lydia and Maria only
suffered what they *deserved*: the consequences were
inevitable, with characters and circumstances like theirs.
She is not concerned with justice, but with facts: content
to draw life, without comment.

Her only personal reflection upon the moral issues
involved,—one of the very few cases in which as author
she interrupts her narrative—reveals an almost startling
independence of thought, an instinctive premonition of
later, more liberal, views.

"That punishment, the public punishment of disgrace,
should in a just measure attend *his* share of the offence
is, we know, not one of the barriers which society gives
to virtue. In this world the penalty is less equal than
could be wished; but without presuming to look forward
to a juster appointment hereafter, we may fairly consider a man of sense, like Henry Crawford, to be providing
for himself no small portion of vexation and regret;
vexation that must rise sometimes to self-reproach, and
regret to wretchedness, in having so requited hospitality,
so injured family peace, so forfeited his best, most
estimable, and endeared acquaintance, and so lost the

woman whom he had rationally as well as passionately
loved."

One detail, in this matter, may perhaps be noticed, as
indicating a somewhat curious convention; surviving,
one must suppose, from the crude distinction between
the classes so boldly illustrated by an earlier writer; which
led Richardson to assume that Pamela was honoured by
marriage with her seducer, while Clarissa resisted Love-
lace to the last, though correspondents besought the
printer to permit her to relent.

Here, we see, that the Bennets felt that Wickham
must be forced to marry their daughter, though Darcy's
"first object had been to persuade her to leave her present
disgraceful situation ; " and the Bertrams desired Maria
"to leave Mr Crawford." There were still two standards
for different social positions.

There has been a good deal of discussion about Jane
Austen's general attitude towards religion and morality.
Her clergymen, it is said, are in no way conspicuous for
devotion or faith; very little concerned to save souls or
uphold the Church. Her heroines seldom investigate
their own souls, or question their rights to happiness.
The counsellors of youth seem more alert to appearances
and their neighbour's opinions, than to the will of God.
Such general criticism is based on a misunderstanding of
her generation. We have so entirely lost touch with the
atmosphere of universal orthodoxy, or the assumption that
all men are Christians, as to forget that it was once pos-

sible to believe and be virtuous without talking about it.
We have achieved such a confusion of ideals, and set up
so many moral standards, that we approach all spiritual
problems by way of an amateur medical diagnosis, regarding the conscience as an expression of nerves and
complexes.

Jane Austen's morality and faith were not conventional
but instinctive. Most of us still have instincts, though
lacking conviction. We must realise that it was once,
if no longer, possible to be sincerely convinced of "the
truth," to feel for oneself what most people accepted or
assumed, to be sincerely orthodox and honestly virtuous,
without questioning the creed. Such an assumption of
faith was never inconsistent with independent judgment
on individual cases or with liberal and broad-minded
charity in thought. When the occasion arose Jane
Austen never hesitated to criticise the common inter-
pretations of religion, the hypocrisy and narrow-minded-
ness of unthinking convention, the false standards of
society. Only she did not intrude her own opinions or
delay her drama by discussion.

On the other hand the people of her novels, for whom
sympathy and affection are invited, always act in accordance with high principles and firm faith. The Bertrams
and the Crawfords miss their way to happiness; the one
for lack of moral guidance, the other from definite im-
moral influences; both from laxity about religion. It is
the same with Wickham, Willoughby, and William Elliot;
with Lydia and Lucy Steele. Charlotte Lucas sacrifices

an ideal to prudence: Elizabeth felt "the pang of a
friend disgracing herself and sunk in her esteem." When
Isabella "deserted" Morland for the fascinating Captain
Tilney, poor Catherine would never have believed "there
had been such inconstancy, and fickleness and everything
that is bad in the world." Frank Churchill and Jane
Fairfax are found guilty of "a very abominable sort of
proceeding," though excuses may be granted the lady:—
"What has it been but a system of hypocrisy and deceit,
espionage and treachery?"

And this, we must not forget, is a question of morals,
not of convention. Under different circumstances,
Marianne Dashwood's silence upon Willoughby's "intentions" was generously excused. Her mother's extreme delicacy even forbade her to ask whether they were
engaged or not. No one actually knew how much there
was between Elinor and Edward, and Lucy's secret was
well kept. Frank Churchill is permitted "to distinguish
one young woman with persevering attention, while he
really belonged to another"; as Captain Wentworth,
thoughtlessly, wooed two sisters at once. It was want
of frankness Miss Austen could not forgive; the hidden
"motives" of William Elliot, Frank Churchill's "manners
so *very* disengaged."

Here, of course, the offence is comparatively very slight
—in kind or degree; but on all acts of moral, or social,
sin Jane Austen felt deeply and wrote with conviction.
She had, certainly, nothing in her of the fanatic, despite
a passage in the *Letters*, which—most unexpectedly—

reveals her suspicion that weakness may, after all, be lurking in natural reticence and good taste.

One of her nieces, though apparently "attached in a degree quite sufficiently for happiness, to poor Mr A.," had experienced a "surprising great change in her feelings." The young gentleman considered, we are told, that "dancing and other social amusements ought to be eschewed and avoided by Christian people." The young lady "was of a different opinion," and consulted her aunt, who roundly declared that his "expressions would not do"; though "no doubt he will get more lively as he is more with you; he will catch your ways if he belongs to you."

She reminds "dear Fanny" that "his situation in life, family, friends, and, above all, his character, his uncommonly amiable mind, strict principles, just notions, good habits, *all* that *you* know so well how to value, *all* that is really of the first importance,—everything of this nature pleads his cause most strongly. . . .

"And, as to there being any objection from his *goodness*, from the danger of his becoming even evangelical, I cannot admit *that*. I am by no means convinced that we ought not all to be evangelicals, and am at least persuaded that *they who are so from reason and feeling must be happiest and safest*. Do not be frightened from the connection by your brothers having most wit—wisdom is better than wit, and in the long run will have the laugh on her side; and *don't be frightened by the idea of his acting more strictly up to the precepts of the New Testament than others*."

Just because this brief passage is not elaborated into a sermon, but occurs between expressions of humorous delight in her niece's "queer little heart—all that is silly and sensible, commonplace and eccentric, provoking and interesting"; its significance is so great. Goodness in her mind is not enough: "nothing can be compared to the misery of being bound *without* love . . . you *may* never attach another man his equal altogether; but if that other man has the power of attaching you *more*, he will be in your eyes the most perfect."

Nowhere else has Jane Austen so unequivocally spoken her own mind on love and religion. There is nothing stereotyped or indifferent on either topic. These are the sentiments and convictions behind the apparent trivial frivolities of her books: an earnest and practical faith in "all that is really of the first importance," but not matter for idle or smart talk over the tea-table, nor artistically in place within the drama of a pleasant tale.

There is something, maybe, of Jane Austen's niece in Fanny Price, though she always preferred the solid wisdom of Edmund. But she could appreciate Crawford's greater wit; and, but for Maria, would, no doubt, have got more lively as she was more with him; and caught his ways if she belonged to him. There, however, the author's "principles" intervened, and the charming sinner was dismissed.

But we have answered the critics. We see Jane Austen's respect for one endeavouring to "act strictly up to the precepts of the New Testament," and no further doubt can be entertained of her fundamentally serious attitude towards life. "I hope," said Elizabeth, "I never ridicule what is wise and good."

There is one occasion, and one only, on which it is hard to believe that she was quite honestly sincere. Mr Elliot, thought Anne, "certainly knew what was right"; but "she distrusted the past, if not the present. . . . She saw there had been bad habits; *that Sunday travelling had been a common thing.* . . . How could it be ascertained that his mind was truly cleansed?" Yet even here, maybe, we are judging this apparent conventionality by our own week-end liberties; and, after all, the vicarage can scarcely avoid a certain "professional" attitude towards the Sabbath.

It has been noticed that on a certain memorable occasion, when Emma Woodhouse found "some alteration to make in the lacing of her half-boot," she had "a charitable visit to pay to a poor sick family," and on "approaching the cottage, all idle topics were superceded. Emma was very compassionate; and the distresses of the poor were as sure of relief from her personal attention and kindness, her counsel and her patience as from her purse. She understood their ways, could allow for their ignorance and their temptations, had no romantic expectations of extraordinary virtue from those for whom education had done so little, entered into their troubles with ready sympathy, and always gave her assistance with as much intelligence as goodwill. In the present instance it was sickness and poverty which she came to visit; and after remaining there as long as she could give comfort and advice, she quitted the cottage with such an impression of the scene as made her say to Harriet, as they walked away—

"These are sights, Harriet, to do one good. How trifling they make everything else appear! I feel now as if I could think of nothing but these poor creatures all the rest of the day, and yet who can say how soon it may all vanish from my mind?"

The words are the words of a patroness: the episode is but a prelude to the entirely frivolous match-making for the egregious Elton; but serious thoughts *would* intervene, which are assuredly the author's own. So expressed, moreover, they reveal Jane Austen, the Vicar's daughter, who visited the parish—not merely from duty, but as a real, if condescending, friend: welcome because she sympathised and understood. Like others of her generation, she had been put out to nurse in the village, and a childhood's familiarity with cottage life would obviously tend to promote a "natural" equality of manner with humble folk.

We remember, too, Emma's smiling confession, at sight of the young cleric, that such impressions might, after all, be quickly banished by more agreeable thoughts :—
"I hope it may be allowed that if compassion has produced exertion and relief to the sufferers, it has done all that is truly important. If we feel for the wretched enough to do all we can for them, the rest is empty sympathy, only distressing to ourselves."

Practical as ever, Jane Austen will not deceive us by
false sentiment; but she could laugh at herself with a
good conscience, because her compassion was honest and
sincere. Happiness may help more than tears; and she
who loved her friends so greatly, was a great friend to all
mankind.

The "outward wretchedness" of that "detached
cottage down Vicarage Lane, the still greater within,"
was placed, artistically, among the wanderings of
Harriet's silly heart; but it serves also to refute Miss
Mitford's thoughtless character of the artist—a husband-
hunting butterfly, here revealed true daughter of the
church. The novel, however, in her opinion is not
concerned with these things and they are never elsewhere discussed; though it may be remarked that both
Henry Tilney and Edmund Bertram "understood the
duty of a parish priest."

"A parish," declared Sir Thomas, "has wants and
claims which can be known only by a clergyman con-
stantly resident, and which no proxy can be capable of
satisfying to the same extent. Edmund might, in the
common phrase, do the duty of Thornton—that is, he
might read prayers and preach—without giving up
Mansfield Park; he might ride over every Sunday, to
a house nominally inhabited and go through Divine
Service; he might be the clergyman of Thornton Lacey
every seventh day, for three or four hours, if that would
content him. But it will not. He knows that human
nature needs more lessons than a weekly sermon can

convey; and that if he does not live among his parish-
ioners, and prove himself, by constant attention, their
well-wisher and friend, he does very little either for their
good or his own."

The baronet had to confess, in after years, that he
had sadly neglected his own daughter's religious education; but he knew what was right, and—in an age of
pluralists—his son unhesitatingly agreed. When Ben-
jamin Lefroy was examined for ordination, we are told,
the Bishop asked him two questions:—Was he the son
of Mrs Lefroy of Ashe: had he married a Miss Austen?
If no more moral, or intellectual, qualities were usually
in demand, we can only admire the more so conscien-
tious a parish priest.

CHAPTER III

MARRIAGE

"I consider a country-dance as an emblem of marriage. Fidelity and complaisance are the principal duties of both; and those men who do not choose to dance or marry themselves have no business with the partners or wives of their neighbours."

A difficulty has been felt, and expressed, on Elizabeth's behalf, in "reconciling" the incompatible truths about Darcy's criticism of the Bennet family, "with a decent respect for them and her father in particular":—

"No other solution can be found of this problem, unless it be in Jane Austen's belief in the overmastering power and the sufficiency of love. In her philosophy love prevails over prudence, family feeling, social conditions, worldly propriety. When love comes in at the door all other considerations fly out of the window. Wickham and Willoughby would have been forgiven if they had been true lovers; they are condemned because they are poor creatures, led by appetite, ambition or avarice, not victims of high passion; such natures do not approach the sanctity of love between two equal and exalted spirits. She has no condemnation for Marianne Dashwood. . . . To her mind the call of love, which comes to few, ought not to be resisted, cannot be resisted, when it comes; and this high-flown sentiment is all the more interesting because all her sentiments are in accordance with common sense."

So complete a reversal of the accepted view, originated by Sir Walter Scott, that Elizabeth accepted Darcy to become the Mistress of Pemberley, that Miss Austen's views on marriage were conventional, a little mercenary, and entirely prosaic, can hardly, I fear, be justified by the evidence.

But, on the other hand, Scott's somewhat bald assertion is manifestly unjust, alike to the novelist and her heroines. It is written of a lady in *Pride and Prejudice* that "without thinking highly either of men or matrimony, marriage had always been her object; it was the only honourable provision for well-educated young women of small fortune, and however uncertain of giving happiness, must be their pleasantest preservative from want." In precisely the same spirit, and from the same point of view, Emma explains that "she has none of the usual inducements to marry."

" Without love, I am sure I should be a fool to change such a situation as mine. Fortune I do not want, employment I do not want, consequence I do not want ; I believe few married women are half as much mistress of their husband's house as I am at Hartfield ; and never, never, could I expect to be so truly beloved and important ; so always first and always right in any man's eyes as I am in my father's."

Love is at least admitted to be important, even essential, to an ideal marriage, but Emma can afford to be independent.

" I shall not be a poor old maid, and it is poverty only which makes celibacy contemptible to a generous public. A single woman with a very narrow income must be a ridiculous, disagreeable old maid—the proper sport of boys and girls ; but a single woman of good fortune is always respectable, and may be as pleasant as anybody else."

There is, after all, very little romance or idealism here; and there *is* a difficulty in reconciling this cold and assured statement of one law for the rich and another for the poor, with the quiet, strong feeling of the lovers in every novel; above all, with the passionate eloquence of Anne Elliot on the fidelity of women. In her letters, again, Jane Austen expressly advises her niece that happiness can only be secured by love, and is doomed to fail in a loveless marriage with the most suitable young man, of the strictest integrity and reasonably handsome, whom you are actually tempted to accept. She will not even commiserate an impecunious couple—"money will come you know, because they cannot do without it."

From our modern standpoint it must be confessed that, in this matter, Jane Austen takes up a middling view; but there is no occasion to doubt her depth of feeling or her faith in the efficacy of love. Charlotte Lucas was cast off without hesitation for a *mariage de convenance*.

Much must be allowed, in our judgment, for Miss Austen's determined reticence, dictated by her conception of moral taste. She was also influenced here, as in all her expressions of sentiment, by her profound dislike and contempt for the rhapsodies of romance, the

high-flown sentimentalities of forced and artificial exalta-
tion, in which the novels she made it her business to
laugh out of court and then seriously reform, universally
abound.

Roughly speaking, fiction reflects the thought and
manner of the age to which it belongs; and when the
modern novel was inaugurated in England the wild-
oats theory of marriage was practically universal,
frankly accepted by Fielding and Smollet; and Richardson was quite definitely in advance of his time, though
rather from his general preference for virtue than from
any particular understanding of the perfect comrade
which is the true lover. To allow your hero a good crop
of wild oats, really involved a vague and slipshod conception of some mysterious affinity with the heroine;
who loved him as it were by telepathic sympathy without
any knowledge whatever of his real character or nature,
and for whom he deceived himself into supposing that
he cherished her image with unwavering fidelity, despite
the weakness of the flesh; and that his love for her was
in some mysterious fashion, he never attempted to
analyse or define, entirely different from, and on a
higher plane than, the passing infatuations which
actually occupied his thoughts, engaged his time, and
formed his pleasures. This was little better than a
modern variation on the frankly artificial gallantries of
the mediæval Courts of Love; no less distasteful to
Jane Austen, in its false idealism, than the vapid
moonings of romance.

When women began to write fiction they immediately disclosed part of the truth about their real feelings on this subject, always professedly more their concern than men's. In the first place they taught us that "nothing will destroy the sense of reality in the average woman . . . that even the greatest, noblest, tenderest love in a woman does not necessarily exclude all practical considerations, all links with everyday reality."

Shakespeare, indeed, divined the truth, but lesser men did not perceive or forgot. When Juliet has selected a trysting-place for the morrow:—

" She reminds Romeo of the time and their danger of discovery, and in almost every word seems to attempt to capture and subdue the winged dream of the lover which is sailing beyond the limits of time and space so that she may reduce it to the common measure of earthly happiness."

Fanny Burney had little philosophy in her nature and was not given to analysis; but she wrote frankly as a woman, for women; and she taught us another truth that whatever we may suppose, however we may flatter ourselves to the contrary, good women prefer the noble Orville to Sir Clement and Mortimer Delvile to Sir Robert; whether or no the stronger sex laugh at virtue and look down on the virtuous. She scattered wild oats to the wind.

Jane Austen carries both these new truths into her own ideals and her work. What she distrusted, however, more consciously than Fanny Burney, was the sudden, instinctive, certainty of love at sight, without the smallest opportunity of testing or understanding the beloved or herself. Marianne, alone among her heroines, "did not require a second interview to be convinced," and she "was born to discover the falsehood of her own opinions."

Though neither Fanny Price nor Anne Elliot were slow to discover a decided partiality which in fact lasted through life, they were not eagerly or blindly impulsive; and founded their expectation of happiness upon a clear and reasonable judgment of probabilities. Never enslaved to a handsome exterior or mere charm of manner, each chose her man for real worth and congenial nature. Catherine had no choice in the matter. For all practical purposes, he was the first man she had ever met—luckily one of the best. Elizabeth began with a little antipathy; Emma had no suspicion of the truth about her heart; both had already been superficially attracted by another.

"I am now convinced," said Miss Eliza, "that I have never been much in love, for had I really experienced that pure and elevating passion, I should at present detest his very name, and wish him every evil. But my feelings are not only cordial towards *him*, they are even impartial towards Miss King. . . . . There can be no love in all this. . . . My sisters take his defection more to heart than I do. They are young in ways of the world, and are not yet open to the mortifying conviction that handsome young men must have something to live on as well as plain."

Emma proves herself to be no less sensible and intelligent.

3

" ' I certainly must,' she said, ' this sensation of listless-ness, weariness, stupidity, this disinclination to sit down and enjoy myself, this feeling of everything being dull and insipid about the house—I must be in love ; I should be one of the oddest creatures in the world if I were not—for a few weeks at least. . . .' Emma continued to entertain no doubt of her being in love. Her ideas only varied as to how much. At first she thought it was a good deal. Afterwards but little."

How perfectly Miss Austen understands the difference between these idle flutterings of harmless inclination, and the deep steady happiness of perfect comradeship and understanding. She believes in love following friendship, gradually growing in certainty and strength, as the two come together with tested sympathy and understanding, each sure at a word of all the other is thinking and feeling, and even where they may not agree, still confident of giving no offence, risking no dispute.

In the extreme case, Emma had known Knightley inti-mately from childhood, he was almost a brother to her; and "in spite of all her faults, she knew she was dear to him; might she not say very dear?"

But " till now that she was threatened with its loss, she had never known how much of her happiness depended upon being *first* with Mr Knightley, first in interest and affection. Satisfied that it was so, and feeling it her due, she had enjoyed it without reflection ; and only in the dread of being supplanted, found how inexpressibly important it had been. . . . From family attachment and habit, and thorough excellence of mind, he had loved her, and watched over her from a girl, with an endeavour to improve her, and an anxiety for her doing right, which no other creature had at all shared."

"My child," cried Mr Bennet, for once in his life roused to a sense of responsibility towards one of his children, "let me not have the grief of seeing *you* unable to respect your partner in life. . . . I know your disposition, Lizzy, I know that you could be neither happy nor respectable unless you truly esteemed your husband."

It has been further hinted that Jane Austen allows us to believe that even a heroine, who is of course only a woman after all, could be satisfied with a second best. No one, indeed, is actually confronted with the problem, unless we consider Brandon a poor substitute for Willoughby, as he certainly was not; for even covering the clear indications that Fanny might have been happy with Henry Crawford, I contend that he was—save for bad luck—more of a man than her estimable cousin.

The reasonable and respectable marriage, to escape poverty in old age, where there has been no ideal sacrificed or loss, presents rather a different issue. Marriage is here clearly an escape from known evils and discomfort, if not actual distress; which were by no means imaginary and "not quite so much against the candour and common sense of the world as appears at first, for a very narrow income has a tendency to contract the mind and sour the temper," as Emma shrewdly observes. Again unmarried women were, and for that matter sometimes still are, dependent upon a family income which ends with their mothers' life, and there were few chances of

earning a living in Jane Austen's day. She has shown
us something of what it meant to teach in school or companion a fractious invalid, in "the most liberal and
elegant establishment of all Mrs Elton's acquaintance
. . . almost equal to Maple Grove."

Both points of view are, perhaps, most clearly stated,
with swift emphasis and compactness, in *The Watsons.*

" I would rather do anything than be a teacher at a school.
I have been at school, Emma, and know what life they lead ;
you never have. I should not like marrying a disagreeable man
any more than yourself ; but I do not think there *are* many
very disagreeable men : I think I could like any good-humoured
man with a comfortable income. I suppose my aunt brought
you up to be rather refined ? "

For precisely similar reasons, Miss Austen would have
faced facts, as Emma faced them for Harriet Smith,
welcoming the fidelity of a Robert Martin when her
obscure parentage had been disclosed and other reasons
convinced her that the girl had no right to any higher
ambitions. Harriet was far too susceptible to make a
happy spinster, and the natural daughter of a decent
tradesman was the "luckiest creature in the world to
have created so steady and persevering an affection in
such a man." There could be "no doubt of her happiness with any good-tempered husband," and she had
secured more than she deserved.

There is a touch of prose, distasteful to the romantic
idealist, in so much practical common sense; but, like
other conventions and rules for conduct, it does not

really hamper independence and is no way inconsistent with absolute sincerity, genuine and passionate emotion, eternal constancy or, if circumstances require it, heroic self-sacrifice. Miss Austen seems a little calm and cool, because she has no notion of dragging ordinary people up to a strenuous ideal, expecting a stupid or frivolous girl to see visions and yearn for abstract perfection. She only wants them all to do their best, and secure permanent happiness, which cannot be secured by unloving luxury or calculated prudence, with the men most suited to their temperament and their taste.

CHAPTER IV

CULTURE

"*I may boast myself to be, with all possible vanity, the most unlearned and uninformed female who ever dared to be an authoress.*"

Miss Austen is writing to poor Mr Clarke, the estimable librarian of Carlton House, who had begged her to invent a clergyman with an enthusiastic turn of mind. Foiled here, he suggests "the august House of Coburg," and she declares: "I could not sit seriously down to write a serious romance under any other motive than to save my life; and if it were indispensable for me to keep it up and never to relax into laughing at myself or at other people, I am sure I should be hung before I had finished the first chapter." Yet in sober earnest, it would be idle to pretend that Jane Austen was, properly speaking, a woman of culture, or even well-read. Musicians and painters, indeed, are seldom literary or learned, but we expect the writer, and emphatically a writer of novels, to reveal peculiar sympathy with the art of letters, an intimate affection for his native "classics," and reliable knowledge of many things.

There is, indeed, an altogether delightful exposure of Queen Elizabeth "by a partial, prejudiced, and ignorant historian" in *Love and Friendship*, which discloses a rather better informed view of history than Catherine Morland's; but Miss Austen was guilty of an unfortunate comment upon the *Spectator*, and her literary criticism can scarcely be called acute. Crawford's enthusiasm for Shakespeare was more dramatic than literary; the conventional "accomplishment" of an agreeable young man, inspired by vanity and a natural gift of elocution. Marianne Dashwood's taste, like Captain Benwick's, was purely emotional; while if Anne and Elinor might "venture to recommend a larger allowance of prose in daily study," it was but to "mention such works of our best moralists, such collections of the finest letters, such memoirs of characters of worth and suffering as occurred to them at the moment." They, too, only read "all such works as heroines must read to supply their memories with quotations." Ladies who "read those enormous great stupid thick quarto volumes which one always sees in the breakfast parlour there, must be acquainted with everything in the world. I detest a quarto. Captain Pasley's book is too good for their society. They will not understand a man who condenses his thoughts into an octavo."

Once, indeed, she sought to protect herself against *ennui*, and to provide her "share of the conversation" by "laying in a stock of intelligence " :—

"I am reading Henry's *History of England*, which I will repeat to you in any manner you may prefer, either in a loose, desultory, unconnected stream, or, dividing my recital as the historian himself divides it himself, into seven parts: the Civil and Military; Religion; Constitution; Learning and Learned Men; Arts and Sciences; Commerce, Coins, and Shipping; and Manners. So that for every evening in the week there will be a different subject. The Friday's lot—Commerce, Coins, and Shipping—you will find the least entertaining, but the next evening's portion will make amends. With such a provision on my part, if you will do yours by repeating the French Grammar, and Mrs Stent will now and then ejaculate some wonder about the cocks and hens, what can we want?"

Of Miss Austen's deep love for books, and her acute theories on fiction, I must speak elsewhere. We have now to discover by what means she produced literature without being literary; how she became an artist without studying art.

Though tending to over-emphasise its academic aspect, the accepted definition of culture should stand. Words mean what they are generally supposed to mean, and should be used as they are generally used. But there is something akin to culture, which maybe no one word can express, that Genius may possess and cultivate with unflagging zeal. That is, a thorough knowledge and understanding, inspired by taste, of individual human beings and their interpretation of life. No artist could be more severe towards himself than Jane Austen, could impose upon himself more exacting standards, or limit himself more strictly within the narrow circle of which her mastery was sure.

Of one small detail, which yet also implies much, she has given us by chance a clear and unhesitating ultimatum. Criticising the manuscript novel of a niece, she writes that "we," *i.e.* Cassandra and herself, "think you had better not leave England. Let the Portmans go to Ireland; but as you know nothing of the manners there, you had better not go with them. You will be in danger of giving false representations. Stick to Bath and the Foresters. There you will be quite at home."

Miss Austen herself applied this principle to every stroke of her pen; not only in respect of place. For which reason her certainty of touch and firm outlines never falter. The ingenious care with which she avoids direct narrative when approaching the unfamiliar, allowing one of her characters to recall the past or describe the absent, is continually revealed afresh, the more closely we study her work. She never "goes with" her characters, where she herself has not been; never invades any subject or any part of life, outside her own experience. She could leave "Italy, Switzerland, and the South of France," to Mrs Radcliffe, without regret.

Here, of course, the most striking omission is marked by her almost complete silence about London, save in casual allusion. The whole characteristic scene of Miss Bingley's formal call in the city and Jane's visit to the Gardiners is narrated by letter, not carried on before the reader. We hear of Harriet Smith in a "box at Astley's"; but Jane Austen was not there. We are not allowed to accompany either Darcy or Mr Bennet in their search for the wicked couple. It is true that Marianne and Elinor spent some unhappy weeks in Berkeley Street with Mrs Jennings—to gaze on "the ivory, the gold, and the pearls" of the toothpick case designed for Robert Ferrars. But the essential features of this period : Marianne's "agony of despair and hope"; her "God God! Willoughby," at the party; and Mrs Jennings' consoling "dried cherries," could have taken place, with equal effect, in any market town. No other "heroine" ever enters "this scene of dissipation and vice."

Miss Austen herself saw Mr Kean as Shylock at Drury Lane, and the *Letters* include gay comments upon her visits to brother Henry, in various parts of the Town; but she dared not venture the "rash step" of paying a call when not expected, "for if the Pearsons were not at home, I should inevitably fall a sacrifice to some fat woman who would make me drunk with small beer." She hopes her "father will be so good as to fetch home his prodigal daughter from town, unless he wishes me to walk the hospitals, enter at the Temple, or mount guard at St James's."

She did not "know" London, as Fanny Burney knew it, like a Londoner; and therefore left the place alone.

Of other limitations, she has been too hastily accused. In Miss Mitford's wish that she had shown "a little more taste, a little more perception of the graceful," we hear the voice of the spinster—an excess of feminine refinement. The doubt whether Darcy is always quite the gentleman, is but one example of misjudgment by standards of a later time. Neither in fiction nor history, as read in diaries or letters, were the early generations "quite" modern gentlemen. Greater formality and more stately conversation was invariably less delicate in the subtleties of thought and phrase.

Another quality, the patience which can alone achieve perfection, has been fortunately revealed by the publication of a cancelled chapter in *Persuasion*. The casual assumption of our comparatively uncritical progenitors, that Jane Austen miraculously produced her best at a first attempt, that *Pride and Prejudice* was as great as anything she ever wrote, must be abandoned without regret. Miracles do not encourage art.

The truth is that, like most writers, she did achieve certain detached supremacies of the kind that are commonly born out of Genius before contact with practice and experience. There is a touch of Spring in Elizabeth Bennet, an abandon of joy in Lady Catherine and Mr Collins, she could—naturally—never recover in more mature work. But, on the other hand, critical analysis may not doubt that her technique steadily advances with each novel, and not only technique. *Persuasion* is deeper than any of its predecessors, more faultless in phrase, more skilfully constructed, more finished in every view.

Yet here the work of a chapter we could praise without qualification from any great writer—was put aside, remodelled to finer perfection in every detail.

Miss Austen, in fact, reveals the best part of culture,

insight and knowledge, within her sphere; and a supreme understanding of the relations between words and thoughts; with humour of the heart and intellectual wit. Hers was no rugged, untamed art; no wide-eyed baby-vision of intuitive, poetic, imagination : which may achieve uncultured literature.

Yet her detachment from the influence of training or opportunity remains unique. Among the pioneer women novelists, Fanny Burney was rich in one kind, George Eliot in another. Jane Austen evolved herself.

From the first, though never in touch with any members of the profession, she wrote confidently as a professional; that is, for the public. There can, I think, clearly have been no doubt, no hesitation, in her immediate determination to turn author, to use her gifts for a career, not a hobby. It was convention, not her private desires, that wrote "By a Lady" on the title-page of *Sense and Sensibility*. Miss Burney's triumph had not yet quite established the view that novel-writing became a lady. But when "the secret had spread so far as to be scarcely the shadow of a secret," she believes "I shall not even attempt to tell lies about it. I shall rather try to make all the money than all the mystery I can of it. People shall pay for their knowledge if I can make them." And her profits were put on record.

Apart from the actual table of figures now published with her "Plan for a Novel," we read in July 1813:—

"Every copy of *Sense and Sensibility* is sold, and has brought me £140, besides the copyright; if that should ever be of any value. I have now, therefore, written myself into £250, which only makes me long for more." It would be interesting to conjecture how much "more" the said copyright has actually "brought in."

The family, indeed, were scribblers, but frankly amateur; and, as a child, she scribbled with the rest. But there was no transition stage, no finding her feet, between the quite undistinguished charades printed with those by other Austens, or the ordinary girl-dramas in Mr Austen-Leigh's *Life*, and the assured finish or technique of *Northanger Abbey*; an experiment from one aspect, but the experiment of an maturely professional novelist. There are, certainly, amateur—or careless—details in *Love and Friendship*, but these are intentional, not immature. Hard labour was out of place, for one always governed by practical common sense, in writing for her friends; and at times the mistake deliberately heightened the caricature.

Her preparation was of another kind, based on critical acumen and personal love; without a debt to "suffering" or isolation. By happy chance, her family did everything to encourage inspiration; thus indirectly helping her to train her powers, to exercise her wit. They devoured books, chatted continually about their friends, "cared" infinitely for each other. And knowing herself, Jane transformed their gay understanding of life and men into art.

It may be difficult for some to believe, and an offence

to others; but I am convinced that she herself owed nothing whatever to poetry or the arts. She indulged her heroines in these things; because she knew that some young ladies really enjoyed Cowper, could talk intelligently of "foregrounds, perspectives, and the picturesque," or practise the piano without fatigue. Miss Bingley's folly had not diminished her respect for the truly "accomplished," the cynicism of Lady Susan had not tempted her to despise education. Miss Weston and Edmund Bertram knew how to guide the industry of intelligent youth; and "reasonable men" do not admire "imbecility in females."

On the other hand, Jane Austen owed everything to books; those books "in which the greatest powers of the mind are displayed, in which the most thorough knowledge of human nature, the happiest delineation of its varieties, the liveliest effusions of wit and humour, are conveyed to the world in the best chosen language." Delight in the most naïve or extravagant romance, growing intimacy with her favourite authors, soon taught her to discern their faults, to mark their disloyalty to real life. She felt no ambition towards new forms of fiction, no desire for aggressive originality: content once more, on questions of right or breeding, to accept the way of convention. But she distrusted types: heroine, villain, confidante, "absent cousin," and the rest. She longed, as Richardson and Fielding with less courage and insight had for themselves determined, to put the breath of life into these pen-puppets, to reincarnate these dearly beloved children of imagination, as men and women of the hearth. True love is never blind, and she resolved to tell what she knew. Fanny Burney had made books from life; Jane Austen made life from books : achieving greater realism by methods less realistic.

I believe that one very important secret of Miss Austen's methods has been disclosed by the recent issue of *Sanditon*, the book on which she was engaged at her death. This is not rejected work, like *Lady Susan*, which, though complete, she chose never to print; or *The Watsons*, which dissatisfaction led her to leave undone. The sentence of the Court, from judge or author, has not been pronounced.

But I cannot accept the description usually given of this manuscript, now inscribed on the official reprint. It is not, I believe, the "Fragment of a Novel," but the "*Fragment of a Synopsis for a Novel.*" We have, also recently, been given the full text of her "Plan for a Novel," in part suggested, no doubt, by the Prince Regent's sedate librarian, Mr Clarke; and *Sanditon* is not the "first draft" of the opening chapters, but a skeleton or careful plan. In advising her "niece" novelist, she wished her to first collect her characters in a quiet neighbourhood; and there, too, she herself must have thought out her *dramatis personæ*, partly at least in groups; building a plot from combined "fiction" and observed types, naturally brought together by the ordinary combinations of real life. To a large extent, her emotion was given to the created, human personalities; her wit and humour to the borrowed children of fiction—and, of course, to incident or situation.

This distinction may be most clearly recognised in *Sanditon*; because here the two elements, or classes of character, still stand apart, side by side but detached; not yet cunningly interwoven by her matchless constructive art.

We have, for example, Sir Edward Denham, "a dangerous man quite in the line of the Lovelaces." He exists for "seduction." He "knew his business," and Clara's "situation in every way called for it." His character had been formed by "all the most exceptionable parts of Richardson," and his ideas are developed by the constant study of the "Genius, Fire and Feeling of the villain of the story."

The biting analysis, every phrase of the description, however keen the wit, are *not* passages from a Jane Austen novel, but scaffolding for the architect. Sir Edward, I am convinced, will play his part, incidently perhaps, or maybe with startling dramatic effect in making difficulties between heroine and hero, the latter, I think, not yet introduced. But he will remain throughout a book-made figure, a remorseless satire, not on man, but on art.

On the other hand, Clara herself, as yet unveiled, may prove a second Jane Fairfax: as kindly and firmly drawn, but probably less heavily burdened with a

domestic conscience, as she certainly seems less heavily
over-weighted with domestic encumbrances. She may,
of course, prove to be the heroine herself; though, by
all Jane Austen rules, the observant, and slightly cynical,
Chatlotte Heywood seems better equipped for the part.
Already a kindly fate has introduced her to a wider
circle of acquaintance than her estimable parents had
ever known. Not having confined their family within
"reasonable limits," they could not afford a "gentleman-
like share of luxuries and change. *They* staid at home,
that their children *might* get out." Charlotte is now
"out"; how and where to get "settled," alas! we shall
never know.

We see the "great" Lady Denham, destined to sit for
a second Lady Catherine, with the manners of Mrs
Norris—but to the last a "novel person"; as are the
invalid group, subtly contrasted with the "good
Parkers," themselves no less foolish and funny, but real
or human in every thought and word.

The style, also, of this so-called "Fragment" is clearly
a form of notes, not of composed narrative. There is
abundance of witty or humorous phrase, for Jane
Austen's thoughts were frequently born of laughter;
but there is not even any attempt at the swift, smooth,
orderly movement of words, often found even in *Love
and Friendship*, and invariably achieved in purposeful
composition. Precision and conciseness are here re-
placed by jerks; emphasis by italics and capital letters;
rapid narrative by a kind of short-hand, or telegraphic,

language. Many a happy turn of subtle character-revelation has been conceived and would no doubt be retained; but I do not believe there is one whole paragraph, scarcely a complete sentence, that she would print as it stands. She must re-write, not revise.

In another sense, *Sanditon* suggests a most tantalising conjecture. It has been most rashly hinted that Jane Austen may have written herself out; or, alternatively, that had she produced another masterpiece, it would still have remained within the strictly defined limits on which she appears to have been always content to work.

But here, for the first time, one of her leading gentlemen is almost entirely absorbed in commercial speculation. Mr Parker's resolve, in season and out of season, to develop his little seaside resort, clearly threatens to fill a large part of her canvas. Now Miss Austen has given us several efficient business men; but she has not, hitherto, allowed them to talk about their work. One might call Mrs Norris a business woman; but her methods of profiteering were not quite the methods of trade. But Lady Denham is Parker's partner, frankly and unashamed.

Again, the "chilly and tender half-mulatto," Miss Lambe, is a new type; the first example of character developed by race. There are other West Indians, "as helpless and indolent as wealth and a hot climate are apt to make us." Miss Lambe a little reminds us of Thackeray's good-natured Miss Schwartz; but we wonder where this may lead. Should she be meant for a leading

lady, Miss Austen must certainly have had in mind fresh
fields for conquest.

The Watsons may be regarded as simply a false start.
The preparation, indeed, is common to almost all her
tales: the refined sisters in a vulgar family group, the
inefficient parent, the "great house," the "reverend"
hero, and the envious gossips. But she must soon have
recognised the risk of sailing too near some of the old
plots. Most conspicuously Lady Osborne could scarcely
have escaped from imitation of the de Burgh, the foreshadowed duel of wits with Emma Watson must have
carried us far too near the "prettyish kind of little
wilderness," at Longburn, where Lady Catherine once
begged the favour of Elizabeth's company, and spoke
her mind. We have the *two* refined sisters from *Pride
and Prejudice*, and an identical vulgarity (without the
excuse of Mrs Bennet) to complete the uncomfortable
majority of daughters. We have the "great people," as
at Netherfield and Barton Park, whose appearance must
"give" a credit "to any assembly . . . for great people
have always their charm." Mr Edwards could really
have taken no more interest than Mr Allen in the young
people's partners, "as he had been fixed the whole time
at the same table in the same room, with only one change
of chairs."

Mr Austen-Leigh, when first printing *The Watsons*,
suggested that it was abandoned because "the author
became aware of the evil of having placed her heroine
too low, in such a position of poverty and obscurity as,

though not necessarily connected with vulgarity, has a sad tendency to degenerate into it. . . . Certainly she never repeated such an error by placing the heroine of any subsequent work under circumstances likely to be unfavourable to the refinement of a lady." This seems to ignore the visits of Fanny Price to Portsmouth, of Marianne to Mrs Jennings, and Mrs Elton's intolerable patronage of Jane Fairfax. I would venture, however, to suggest a slight variant of this view, which is possibly also more consistent with the facts.

As a perfect lady, Miss Austen was doubtless averse to class *mixtures*; except for dramatic effects—as when confronting Henry Crawford with Mrs Price, driving Anne Elliot to Westgate Buildings, and submitting Elinor Dashwood to the vulgar insinuations of Lucy Steele. And her taste might well have revolted against a plot constructed upon such social incongruities, equally false to life and art.

Some materials from *The Watsons* were "used in another fabric," chiefly at Donwell and Randalls, where, we may note, she kept, even more rigidly than in other novels, to one class. No one in Highbury could ever have found occasion to study Sir Walter Elliot's favourite volume. The neighbourhood could not boast either a baronet or a general. Even the "officers" passed it by. The "Woodhouses were first in consequence *there*"; yet equally at home with Knightley or Miss Bates.

Emma Watson gained much by her "rise" to Emma Woodhouse, and dropping both her refined and "impossible" sisters; and Lady Catherine was far happier, without the romantic tenderness for Mr Howard, which lent an unwanted pathos to Lady Osborne.

But the air of Highbury can be seen plainly stirring in *The Watsons*. The first Emma's father would have his "basin of gruel," for supper, when "the clock struck nine." His selfish invalidism regulates the home life and determines many details of the plot. She is admirable as a daughter; always ready to give him "the gentleness and silence" he demanded when ill, or to "make up" a card-table when he was more socially inclined. Mrs Robert Watson is an anticipated understudy for Mrs Elton, with her "My good creature, use no ceremony with me, I entreat you," her vulgar prattle about the "select parties" at Croydon and the "seven tables" in her "drawing-room," *and* her "dear Mr W."

There is something, I think, of the genial Weston in the "communicative" Mr Edwards, "fresh from the street and ready to tell whatever might interest," because "he had lived long enough in the idleness of a town to become a little of a gossip"; while Robert, like the brothers Knightley, must "understand the last current report as to public news . . . before he could let his attention be yielded to the less rational and important demands of the women."

Elizabeth Watson, like Emma Woodhouse, "would rather do anything than teach in a school"; and her contention that "*it is very bad to grow old and be poor and laughed at*" was elaborated in the later novel, to silence the fears of Harriet Smith. "Never mind, I shall not be a *poor* old maid," said Emma, "*it is poverty only* which makes celibacy contemptible to a generous public."

Jane Austen, we see, did not trust the spontaneous expression of her imaginative wit: she studied the arts of living and writing, she used her brains, she laboured upon technique—to accomplish the mastery of her pen.

It has been happily said that "she knew what every one of her people did yesterday and would do to-morrow, and what had happened, and was going to happen, to make them do it."

CHAPTER V

READING

"You have been studying novels, I suspect," said Sir Edward, enraged at "the manliness of his son's reply."

It has been remarked, with surprise, that there was only "one novel" in Dr Burney's library; and it is clear that whatever training his famous daughter may have received, it was but slightly derived from books. She had exceptional opportunities, paternally encouraged, for the study of mankind, and therein found both inspiration and delight. *Evelina* might have been the first novel ever written in the world, for all consciousness ever revealed by its author of its predecessors. She wrote absolutely out of herself. She knew of novelists and novels, as an actor occasionally remembers the play-writer and the play. Instinctively a public performer in a family of performers—and the friends of performers—she naturally gave the world what she had invented for her own delight. And, with her inherited professional instincts, protested against the injustice commonly dealt out to the professions. But she had never been, and never became, a literary person; save so far as a reputation for wit might prove a social asset.

Jane Austen, on the other hand, was a born reader and

55

lover of books. No scholar or pedant, as we have noted, she yet always regarded authors with respect; and she must have criticised novels almost as soon as she learned to read. It was her love of fiction that tempted her to scribble, before her love for humanity taught her to curb the extravagances and unrealities of romance.

This is the natural course in the development of art; though so often declared the reverse. Many critics have been surprised at her precocity in wit, the maturity of her romance: the cold mind that sparkles in *Northanger Abbey*, the warm heart that beats in *Persuasion*; using their wonder to confirm a mistaken charge of mercenary views on marriage—"that she couldn't understand and couldn't draw the deepest feelings of our hearts."

Miss Clemence Dane finds her suspicions confirmed by *Love and Friendship*:

That " in Jane Austen the usual order of development is reversed. Most people are born with a heart and develop a head ; but Jane seems to have arrived intellectually complete, the late-born child of the age of cold reason, every faculty alert ; but with a heart so fast asleep, so briaed and wintered over by wit, caution, and common sense, that it is a wonder it ever woke at all. That it did wake, to warm like a slow-rising sun her chill and glittering world, the novels show in delicious gradation, as one by one they merge the cruel wit of her childhood in the rich humour of her prime."

I confess that, despite its sound, and exquisitely expressed, appreciation, the deduction appears to me profoundly untrue. Youth, of course, is romantic, or was before the War: it is warm-hearted, generous, and glowing with love for mankind. But art is seldom born out of emotion. Its nursery games are a continual play on words. Drunk with the power, denied the commonality, of the sharp phrase, the flower of eloquence, or the graces of word-music; the young poet is for ever daring new rhythms, the young critic for ever experimenting in beautiful prose, the young dreamer for ever fashioning images of grace and form: his brain at work to achieve the new or worship the old.

In art it is always youth that ignores tender humanity and glories in *Love's Labour Lost*, with its "brilliant unrealities, affectations of dress, of manner, of languages, and of ideas."

It is, indeed, wellnigh bursting with ideas; almost indifferent to feeling.

Miss Austen's *Letters* abound in references to books; nearly all her characters were great readers; though some were foolish, and some wise.

When the "high-brow" Mrs Martin ventured to boast that *her* library would "not consist only of novels, but of every kind of literature," Jane writes: "She might have spared this pretension to *our* family who are great novel-readers, and not ashamed of being so." Her eager enjoyment in every kind of story appears again and again, with reference to long-forgotten novels and books: there is more than one allusion to the family's energy in securing an abundant supply of "something to read." We hear, in January 1813, that "the Miss Sibleys want to establish a Book Society in their side of the country, like ours. What can be a stronger proof of that superiority in ours over the Manytown and Steventon Society, which I have always foreseen and felt? No emulation of the kind was ever inspired by *their* proceedings; no such wish of the Miss Sibleys was ever heard in the many years of that Society's existence. And what are their Biglands and their Barrows, their Macartneys and their Mackenzies to Captain Pasley's *Essays on the Military Police of the British Empire* and *The Rejected Addresses*?"

She judges her friends by their taste in books: "There are two traits in Miss Fletcher's character which are pleasing, namely, she admires *Camilla*, and drinks no cream in her tea."

The evidence with regard to the "persons in the novels" is overwhelming. Marianne Dashwood, of course, carried everything to extremes; but she was nothing if not sincere. Had she a fortune, she "would buy books! Thomson, Cowper, Scott—she would buy them all over and over again—she would buy up every copy to prevent their falling into unworthy hands; and would have every book that tells her how to admire an old twisted tree— and the bulk of her fortune would be laid out in annuities on the authors or their heirs." Miss Austen, you observe, resents the fact that writers are not well-paid.

She could never have given her heart to Willoughby, though he *had* saved her life and was very good-looking, till she had questioned him "on the subject of books, when her favourite authors were brought forward and dwelt upon with rapturous delight. . . . Their taste was strikingly alike. . . . The same books, the same passages were idolised by each. . . . He read with sensibility and spirit."

Darcy *had* the fortune which she only desired, and was "always buying books" for the library at Pemberley, itself "the work of many generations."

Anne Elliot was supposed to have "refused Charles Musgrove because he might not be learned or bookish enough"; Benwick had "a tolerable collection of well-bound volumes," and "considerable taste in reading"; was always talking of "Mr Scott and Lord Byron." He even "turned Louisa into a person of literary taste." Once, it had been "give him a book and he will read all day," in mourning for love lost; now "he sat at Louisa's elbow, reading verses, or whispering to her, all day long."

No matter the temperament of nice people, they must love books.

Edmund Bertram recommended his cousin to books, for her "leisure hours, encouraged her taste, and corrected her judgment." Catherine Morland read Pope, Gray, Thomson, Shakespeare—*and* Mrs Radcliffe.

Though Brandon was over thirty, he "had read, and had a thinking mind." Elinor's spirited defence of Edward's "reading aloud" against the romantic derision of her rapturous sister, is the defence of a book-lover. She "had heard his opinion on subjects of literature and taste," and could pronounce that "his mind was well-informed, his enjoyment of books exceedingly great, his imagination lively, his observation just and correct, and his taste delicate and pure."

Marianne had misjudged him, because she "*would* give him Cowper," and how could she "hear those beautiful lines, which had frequently almost driven her wild, pronounced with such impenetrable calmness, such dreadful indifference. . . . It would have broke *my* heart, had I loved him, to hear him read with so little sensibility."

It is, however, the two Henrys, Crawford and Tilney, who most definitely establish Miss Austen's serious convictions and emotional enthusiasms. As always, Tilney conceals his thoughts with a laugh. After teasing Catherine for pitying the writers of history; he proclaims his pride in the broken "promise" he "made of reading" *Udolpho* aloud to his sister, refusing to "wait only five minutes," stealing "her own copy, particularly her own," and "finishing it in two days, his hair standing on end the whole time." But he "becomes serious at last"; frankly indignant at the affected superiority of the fools who pretend to consider that reading novels is beneath the dignity of men. He assures the delighted girl that he, too, loves Laurentina and all the heroines in the world. He is not ashamed, but proud, to admit it.

Crawford's culture is more directly told. He had only to take up "a volume of Shakespeare, and could fall into the flow of his meaning immediately"; he "gave the sense," and was "truly dramatic?"

" To *good* reading Fanny had been long used ; her uncle read well, her cousins all, Edmund very well, but in Mr Crawford's reading there was a variety of excellence beyond anything she had ever met with. The King, the Queen, Buckingham, Wolsey, Cromwell, all were given in turn ; for with the happiest knack, the happiest power of jumping and guessing, he could always alight at will on the best scene, the best speeches of each ; and whether it were dignity or pride, or tenderness or remorse, or whatever were to be expressed, he could do it with equal beauty."

He and Fanny had "moral and literary tastes in common." I suspect that, in Jane Austen's mind, the two were commonly to be found together.

Negative evidence is no less strong. The people Miss Austen despised, scorned books. John Thorpe is almost more of a fool than Mr Collins or Mr Elton: he is at least more ordinary, dismissed with more caustic brevity. He considered novels "the stupidest things in creation, all so full of nonsense and stuff, the horridest nonsense you can imagine." Miss Bingley is more foolish, in an ordinary way, than Miss Bates; and she was soon "exhausted by the attempt to be amused with her own book, which she had only chosen because it was the second volume of Mr Darcy's."

There is finally no more drastic statement of social distinction, than Emma's summary dismissal of Mr Martin's pretensions, to *her* friend, Harriet Smith. She assumes that he "is not a man of information beyond the line of his own business. He does not read. What has he to do with books."

Poor Harriet is driven to confess that "he never read the *Romance of the Forest* nor the *Children of the Abbey*: even forgetting to obtain them, at her request."

Books are always the test. By them, we see in her *Letters*, she partly placed her friends. By them, in her novels, she separated the sheep from the goats.

CHAPTER VI

EARLY LIFE

Catherine's father was a clergyman, without being neglected or poor, and a very respectable man, though his name was Richard. . . . She could never learn anything before she was taught, and sometimes not even then. . . . Provided that nothing like useful knowledge could be gained from them, provided they were all story and no reflection, she had never any objection to books at all. . . . She was fond of all boy's plays, and greatly preferred cricket, not merely to dolls, but to the more heroic enjoyments of infancy, nursing a dormouse, feeding a canary-bird, or watering a rose-bush. . . . She loved nothing so well in the world as rolling down the green slope at the back of the house."

Dare we read into this description of an unconventional heroine, the picture of Jane Austen's nursery days? The Austens certainly "will be always called a fine family," and "there was not one family among their acquaintance who had reared and supported a boy accidentally found at their door: not one young man whose origin was unknown. . . . But when a young lady is born to be a [novelist], the perverseness of forty surrounding families cannot prevent her."

Catherine, alone among Jane Austen's heroines, grew

up in a crowd of lively brothers, three of them older than herself. Elizabeth had too many sisters; Anne Elliot no more than two; Emma was an only child. Fanny's William has a distinguished place in the plot; and was an obvious tribute to her sailor brothers.

But the determined ordinariness of the Morlands, artistically designed for satire on romance, produces drama, as Jane Austen found it "where nothing ever happens"; and one may regard this compact first chapter of this early novel as an illuminating introduction to the miracle of her art. We do not *know* anything of her childhood, but I am sure Mrs Austen "did not insist on her daughters being accomplished in spite of incapacity or distaste"; and being "much occupied in lying-in," made life fairly free and easy for the young people. Rather than separate the sisters, Jane was sent to school as a mere child; because, as her mother somewhat grimly remarked: "If Cassandra were going to have her head cut off, Jane would insist on sharing her fate."

We can realise her life most clearly from the novels, for, indeed, they are far more real than such fragmentary facts as have come down to us of her material presence. The *Letters* and biographies serve to fill out the scene; not resembling, of course, in plot, her individual experience, but confirming our impressions of her character and thoughts, the quiet and simple people with whom she lived.

"I do not think it worth while," she wrote, "to wait for enjoyment, until there is some real opportunity for it"; but "Kent is the place for happiness. . . . I do not want people to be very agreeable, as it saves me the trouble of liking them a great deal. . . . Pictures of perfection make me sick and wicked."

Born on 16th December 1775, Jane Austen only lived until 18th July 1817; and these forty-two years embrace few significant or dramatic events. We are sometimes inclined to pity her for the monotony and limited range of her existence, the apparent calmness of her emotions. How far she actually was content, we shall, alas! never know.

The family money, we regret to say, was made by trade—in the sixteenth century: later Austens "married into gentility," and her father, George Austen, entered the Church by way of nepotism from cousin Knight of Godersham, thus adding the prestige of the cloth to a grammar school and university breeding. Presented, in 1761, to the living of Steventon near Overton, in Hampshire; he later acquired, by purchase of an uncle, the adjacent rectory of Deane, taking possession in 1773. Residence occurred between these dates, in 1764; on his marriage with Cassandra, niece of Theophilus Leigh, of All Souls. His wife, we read, "was amusingly particular about people's noses, having a very aristocratic one herself."

From both sides, therefore, the universities lent an added poise to the inevitable dignities of a priestly circle in the backwaters of civilisation. Yet none of the Austens, I think, were really heavy or given to pomp.

5

We need not suppose that Mr Bennet was drawn from the handsome rector, whose hair at seventy was milk-white, "with short curls about the ears"; but his humorous understanding with Elizabeth was surely true to life. Mrs Austen, we learn, had "plenty of sparkle and spirit in her talk," could write excellent letters in prose or "playful" rhyming "common sense."

Yet in the main, I suspect, as in most families, the younger generation were sufficient unto themselves. Jane's devotion to Cassandra became a household word and is indubitably established; her love for her sailor-brothers is revealed to us in two of the novels; as the affectionate teaching of the elder James finds an echo in Edmund Bertram; Edward, like Henry Crawford, was "experienced and adroit in planting and screening, or making additions to a house." It was a labour of love; and his affectionate benevolence suggested the warm-hearted and generous hospitality of Sir John Middleton, "a blessing to all the juvenile part of the neighbourhood"; while Henry loyally conducted all her business with publishers. Nor should the various sister-in-laws be left out of the picture. They contributed much to the gaiety of life, were affectionately disposed to the whole family; and so remarkable an instance of a mother and sisters approving of "the men's" wives is reflected in *Pride and Prejudice, Emma,* and nearly all the novels.

In due course, nephews and nieces were added to the merry circle (Edward had twelve children); and here the evidence of the *Letters* and biographies has produced a reversal of judgment against Jane Austen, on a charge of unnatural coldness. It was once assumed that because she complained of noise and roughness from the little Musgroves and almost sneered at Lady Middleton's spoiled darlings, she had no affection for children. But the contrary is now made clear.

Aunt Jane was the general favourite. "She was the one to whom we always looked for help. She could make everything amusing to a child. She would tell us the most delightful stories, chiefly of fairyland, and her fairies had all characters of their own. The tale was invented, I am sure, at the moment, and was continued for two or three days if occasion required—being begged for on all possible and impossible occasions." We have already quoted from the charming series of letters to two nieces, the one on marriage and the other on novel-writing; but there are others of equal understanding to even younger mites. Here again she does not expect Sunday-school virtue or precocious wisdom. Edward's sons from Winchester, we read, "were very attentive to the Psalms and Lessons and a sermon at home; but you will not expect to hear that they did not return to conundrums the moment it *was over*." And when Fanny Knight went "out of conceit" with a new cap directly she brought it home, Jane remarks, "I consider it as a thing of course at her time of life—one of the sweet taxes of youth—to choose in a hurry and make bad bargains?"

This life-long sympathy and affection with a large family is manifestly reflected in her work. For even

writers who had the professionally congenial friendships
she never enjoyed, have seldom been so entirely at one
with the comrades of daily life. Cassandra, pre-emi-
nently, and the rest in varying degree, actually spoke her
own language; Jane pronounced her "the finest comic
writer of the present age." They were as one, not only
at heart but in intellect and wit: a rare experience, indeed, for any woman of genius, so wedded to her art.
They, too, observed, and laughed, and understood, with
almost equal power; only to her was added the gift of
words to tell all she knew. And being secure of their
loyal appreciation, that was not blinded by love, but
shrewd and critical as her own, she was never bitter or
morbid or alone.

Jane came between her two youngest sailor brothers,
born in 1775, two years after Cassandra, and there were
four elder brothers: James, born in 1765; George, an
invalid, in 1766; Edward [Knight], in 1767; and Henry,
in 1771. There was, in fact, the closest natural childhood
intimacy with the boys destined for the Navy, so affectionately recreated from middy to admiral, in William
Price, Frederick Wentworth, and Admiral Croft. Anne
"gloried in being a sailor's wife, but she must pay the
tax of quick alarm for belonging to that profession
which is, if possible, more distinguished in its domestic
virtues than in its national importance."

The girls, perhaps, *were* sent to an "honest, old-
fashioned boarding-school" at Reading "to be out of
the way"; but there is nothing in *Emma* to show that

Jane approved Mrs Goddard's methods of leaving her
pupils to "scramble themselves into a little education."
Harriet Smith was a favourite there; and "What," cried
Knightley, "are Harriet's claims, either of birth, nature,
or education? She is known only as parlour boarder at
a common school! . . . She has been taught nothing
useful!"

Miss Austen has no more respect for such training
than for the finishing governess who taught the Miss
Bertrams "a great deal of mythology, and all the metals,
semi-metals, planets, and distinguished philosophers."
The education she approved was the "well-informed,
useful," Miss Taylor's "sixteen years of kindness,"
Edmund's zeal "in assisting the improvement of Fanny's
mind, and extending its pleasures, encouraging her taste,
and correcting her judgment. He made reading useful
by talking to her of what she read." Henry Tilney's
"instructions," too, "were so clear that Catherine soon
began to see beauty in everything admired by him."
Such were the pleasant hours of study with Jane's own
father and eldest brother; and she knew how to appreciate their value: those of us "who wished to learn
never wanted the means"; and we should remember
that Anne Elliot had "knowledge enough of the language
to translate at sight these inverted, transposed, curtailed
Italian lines, into clear, comprehensible, elegant English."

We know rather more of Jane Austen in her dancing
days, when the *Letters* reveal almost equal power with
the novels for vignette portraiture, and a swift, neat

phrase to express the humours and absurdities of life. She is, indeed, less restrained; because she knew that Cassandra would read behind the apparent cynicism or spite. They had both, for example, met Mrs Stent; who was "always in the way, unequal to anything, and unwelcome to everybody"; and there was no occasion to mention her good qualities. Very possibly Cassandra might feel that Mrs Holder, by "being dead," had *not* "done the only thing in the world she could possibly do to make one cease to abuse her." She might guess that Mrs Hall was *not* "brought to bed of a dead child, some weeks before she expected, because she happened unawares to look at her husband." She probably knew "Mrs Children's two sons, who are to have one wife between them, a Miss Halwell, who belongs to the Black Hole of Calcutta"; and Mrs Blount, looking "exactly as she did in September, with the same broad face, diamond bandeau, white shoes, pink husband, and fat neck."

There were, of course, many women of fashion, "at once expensively and nakedly dressed," to be met at the Assemblies; more than one "Mrs B., who felt herself obliged to leave her party to run round the room after her drunken husband."

Jane's "excellent" plan, when "promoted" housekeeper, of providing her *own* favourite dishes, was obviously a familiar jest; though it may have proved something of a shock to hear that she intended to engage "a steady cook, and a young giddy housemaid, with a sedate, middle-aged man, who is to undertake the double office of husband to the former, and sweetheart to the latter. No children, of course, to be allowed on either side."

But, after all, as Mr Bennet remarked, "For what do we live but to make sport for our neighbours, and to laugh at them in our turn."

On the other hand, Cassandra would certainly dismiss a ball as "very thin," at which "there were thirty-one people, and only eleven ladies."

For us, in any case, it is more important to recall that between the day when Jane decided to refuse Tom Lefroy "unless he promised to give away his white coat," and his aunt's visit to Steventon, without once mentioning his name, three priceless manuscripts had been completed and were even then already in her desk. *Pride and Prejudice*, *Sense and Sensibility*, and *Northanger Abbey* were all completed at Steventon, before their author was twenty-four; in the full bloom of her dancing days. The life of imagination, behind the quizzing and gossip about her neighbours, had already begun; in no way lessening, certainly, her deep affection and keen interest in every detail of family interest; but encouraging, perhaps, a little indifference to mere acquaintances; to whom her occasional fits of silent observation seem to have been rather alarming at times. "A wit, a delineator of character, who does not talk, is terrific indeed," as Miss Mitford somewhat violently remarked; though, "after all, she could not quite vouch for this account."

She once advised a niece, at the age of twelve, to "cease writing until she was sixteen," because "she herself often wished she had read more and written less in the corresponding years of her life," but I rather suspect the warning was more sympathetic than precise as to facts. *Love and Friendship* was written in 1792, at the age of seventeen; and there is no more either of quantity or quality, in the charades, comedies or burlesques, described or quoted in the *Life* than one would expect from any intelligent family at an age when writing-games were in vogue.

Pride and Prejudice belongs to the years 1796 and 1797, when she was already of age; and the rapidity of composition, which produced three novels in two years, is more remarkable than the author's youth.

On the other hand, there is clear evidence of wide reading in *Love and Friendship* and the first novels, as the *Letters* disclose frequent demands on the circulating library.

It does not appear that any secrecy was attempted with the family or among a few intimate friends. Indeed, the eagerness with which she awaits their opinion of each novel, and her delight in their enjoyment of them, are among the most welcome passages in her letters. The plan for a novel contains marginal allusions at every sentence, to the particular person who had supplied each idea.

But, on the other hand, her taste was strong against any parade of authorship, and her affection would have accused herself of both conceit and selfishness, had she required privacy for work, or allowed herself to be so absorbed as to neglect any social or domestic duty.

But thoughts cannot always be controlled, and there are few more charming touches in biography than the reminiscence of an admiring niece. When becomingly engaged with her needle "beside the fire," we are told, "she would suddenly burst out laughing, jump up and run across the room to her desk, write something down, and then come back to the fire and go on quietly working." In that family, none would resent the obvious inference, that she had probably not heard a word they had been saying.

On the other hand, "she was careful that her occupation," when actually at work, should not be suspected by servants or visitors or any persons beyond her own family party. She wrote upon small pieces of paper which could be easily put away or covered with a piece of blotting-paper. There was between the front door and the offices [at Chawton, *i.e.* when the second group were being written] a swing-door which creaked when it opened; but she objected to have this little inconvenience remedied, "because it gave her notice when anyone was coming." Yet the Austens never carried any theory or rule of life beyond the limits of common sense. They changed their minds, on non-essential matters, when convenient; and, in the end, Jane submitted, with good grace, to a mild form of playing the lion; and obviously enjoyed at least the humorous aspect of the experience.

"Oh, I have more of such sweet flattery from Miss Sharp," she writes in 1813, from Godhersham Park, when in possession of "five tables, eight and twenty chairs, and two fires all to herself." "She is an excellent kind friend. I am read and admired in Ireland, too. There is a Mrs Fletcher, the wife of an old judge, an old lady, and very good and very clever, who is all curiosity to know about me—what I am like, and so forth. . . .

"I do not despair of having my picture in the Exhibition at last—all white and red, with my head on one side; or perhaps I may marry young Mr D'Arblay. I suppose in the meantime I shall owe dear Harry a great deal of money for printing, etc."

The closing sentence certainly redeems the writer from any possible suspicion of superiority or conceit.

Meanwhile there is a legend, more or less accredited by her descendants, of possibly sad romance, hovering round these last days at the old home. Little positive evidence, and that little somewhat contradictory, has been given us concerning the love-affair which is supposed to have clouded, at least a part of, her life; and which, to some minds, accounts for the years of mental inactivity between the writing of the first—and second—three novels.

At least we know that "there was a man," clearly attracted and probably attracting, whom Cassandra thought worthy to have engaged her sister's love. Jane herself plainly told her niece that, in such case, worthiness is not enough:—"You are *not* in love with him;

you never *have* been really in love with him"; nor need one wait for wealth; "as to money, that will come, you may be sure, because they cannot do without it"; and always, in any case, "marriage is a great improver."

She was obviously excellent friends with Tom Lefroy—"most profligate and shocking in the way of dancing and sitting down together"—and she thought of him kindly for many years: but there was nothing serious here. Her own references, indeed, to various acknowledged admirers are too veiled by humour for any reliable inference. Of one we read, "He was a piece of perfection, noisy perfection, himself; which I always recollect with regard"; of another, his partiality "will decline away in a very reasonable manner. . . . It is most probable that our indifference will soon become mutual, unless his regard, which appeared to spring from knowing nothing of me at first, is best supported by never seeing me."

We are almost tempted to echo Jane's "entreaty" to Elizabeth that "she would be serious"; but maybe it is better so. It is not really our business.

The general charge, originated by Scott and echoed by Whately, that Miss Austen's ideas of marriage were mercenary and cold, may be dismissed without a doubt. Because Elizabeth *said* that she "must date her love from my first seeing his beautiful grounds at Pemberley," we know this was not the case.

And when she herself wrote of some friends at Portsmouth that "they lived in the most private manner

imaginable, without keeping a servant of any kind:—
What a prodigious innate love of virtue, she must have,
to marry under such circumstances"; we recognise a
reflection the very reverse of what is said.

Miss Bates, we know, was only ridiculous because poor;
and "single women have a dreadful propensity for being
poor, which is one very strong argument in favour of
matrimony."

We shall learn nothing of the truth from either letters
or novels.

Something, no doubt, occurred which held out a reasonable prospect of happiness, in that condition which Jane
Austen firmly believed was the most likely to secure it,
the normal and natural conclusion of human life. But
the impression certainly prevails that her disappointment was not tragic. One cannot tell; because her
courage was high, and she would have counted it sin to
waste the years in regret; to refuse smaller blessings
when the greatest was denied.

But her heroines do not fall violently in love at the
first favourable impression—for them love grows to
depth and intensity, only as intimacy and mutual knowledge is gained, in the best way, after the plighted troth.
That, certainly, was never hers; and we may therefore
suppose that whatever feelings had been awakened, died
a natural and peaceful death, leaving no sting, as the
opportunity to feed them was withdrawn.

I see no need to require such explanation for the pause
in novel-writing. There are two more obvious reasons

for this. *Pride and Prejudice* had been declined by return of post, though publication was offered "at the author's risk": a few years later, *Northanger Abbey* was bought, for ten pounds, by a publisher in Bath who refused to print it; and the enthusiasm which had produced three books in so few years, may well have been discouraged by such a check. It may be, moreover, that, though confident at heart of her powers, she was also modest enough—as, indeed, her nature would manifestly lead one to expect—to consider seriously whether anything could not be done by way of change to please the public. She had written for the public, having a high regard for fiction; and there were, in fact, certain clearly defined modifications in her later work.

It should be further considered that the following years were comparatively unsettled; and, moreover, in another sense disturbed by personal sorrow for the death of her father and an intimate friend. One feels that she was most herself in a permanent home, never secured at Bath, when life was, not necessarily quiet, but moving in ordered, regular lines.

It has, again, been often suggested that the well-known passage on women's fidelity, "when hope is gone," has in it the ring of personal experience. But, in the first place, any hint from life might, with equal or greater probability, have come from Cassandra, whose fiancé *had* died abroad; and, in the second place, *Persuasion* is the most perfectly constructed of all her novels, that is, the most dramatic; where, above all, we may be sure that the sentiments and emotions expressed, whether or no in agreement with the author's, are absolutely those of the characters in the tale, and revealed for that reason only. Here, assuredly, Jane Austen—the artist—could not herself intrude.

CHAPTER VII

LATER LIFE

"*I get more and more reconciled to the idea of our removal. We have lived long enough in this neighbourhood: the Basingstoke balls are certainly on the decline, there is something interesting in the bustle of going away. . . . For a time we shall now possess many of the advantages I have often thought of with envy in the lives of sailors or soldiers.*"

As the day approached, clearly, Jane Austen was somewhat reconciled to the change; determined at least to look on its bright side. An earlier visit to Bath, in search of suitable address, had found her in "two very nice-sized rooms, with dirty quilts and everything comfortable." The jest has once more triumphed over the discomfort.

It was indeed a change; for now the summers were spent in different parts of the country; widening somewhat her knowledge of life and the country, though, so far as we know, the September of 1804 at Lyme Regis was the only visit which has left its mark, with any emphasis, upon her work. Bath, of course, was not new ground. There is more detailed realism of its streets and "prospects" in *Northanger Abbey* than in *Persuasion*; but "dear, sweet Louisa, so eager and so resolute," could never have fallen "on the pavement on the Lower Cobb" had not fate directed the novelist to that "pleasant little bay, animated by bathing machines and company; its old wonders and new improvements." Who knows, then, if she might not have married Captain Wentworth?

At Bath, however, she never "learned to feel at home." The December of 1804 brought news of the death of her great friend, Mrs Lefroy of Ashe; in less than a month George Austen "closed his virtuous and happy life." Her letter to Frank, then on the high seas, has been published—and criticised for its conventional phrasing: without just cause. We have seen how seldom she put emotion into the written word; and this seems to have been a family characteristic.

We do not imagine that any of them had taken deep roots in Bath; and the move to share a house with Francis and his wife at Southampton was a natural step, made the more agreeable by the addition of the latter's sister Martha, long a favourite, and till Mrs Austen's death, absolutely one of themselves.

For a time, indeed, the widow and daughters found themselves "in what must be called straitened circumstances." Mrs Austen writes: "One hundred and forty pounds a year is the whole of my income. My good sons have done all the rest." There was, of course, no distress, and though a certain amount of worry and temporary disappointment was expressed over a legacy the mother had expected and did not, after all, receive; there was no permanent sensitiveness about the help which, among such perfect friends, seemed practically the same as the conventional support every woman expects from her husband.

From "the unmeaning luxuries of Bath and the stinking fish of Southampton," no doubt the Austens were glad to retire once more to a quiet life in the country.

It was, in fact, when Edward, who had taken the name of Knight from the cousin who left him the large estates of Chawton near Alton and Godersham in Kent, offered his mother a cottage near his own Manor House in 1809, that they at last secured a real second home; with its large garden, "a pleasant irregular mixture of hedgerow and gravel and orchard, and long grass for mowing," the shrubbery border "very gay with pinks and sweet williams, peonies, columbine and syringa," the apricot, beech, and mulberry trees; altogether a "pleasant and commodious abode."

There is a strong sense of home in all the letters of this period, while settling in at Chawton. There was now a good deal of care to be taken of Mrs Austen, over seventy years old, and the daughters had taken over the management of the house. Needlework was continued, and we hear of some regular "good works" undertaken, teaching the poor to read or write.

On the other hand, when the Knights were at Chawton House, balls and visiting became the fashion; and if a younger generation were now the leading spirits of the dance, Jane was not the one to damp their gaiety or withdraw from her own share in a livelier existence.

6

Nevertheless, the significance of Chawton is the proof-reading and publication of two from the earlier group of novels; the writing and publication of two from the second group. *Persuasion* was just finished and *Sanditon* begun, at the time of her death: the former to appear with the long-hidden *Northanger Abbey* in the year following; the latter, in its complete form, not till another century had sprung into full life.

"I can no more forget S. and S. than a mother can forget her sucking child," wrote Jane Austen; and, though they are few enough, we have some invaluable references to detail of how intimately her heart and mind were now absorbed in the work; how real to her the people of her tales must have been; and the eagerness with which sisters and nieces and friends watched the progress of each tale, and the slowly awakening interest and rather hesitating praise that followed the issue, in 1811, of *Sense and Sensibility*. A novel. By a Lady. Printed for the author and published by T. Egerton: Whitehall.

It seems that further work was not actually started until this was out of hand, but *Mansfield Park* had evidently passed its opening stages before *Pride and Prejudice* appeared, in 1813, if not before its revision, from the original "First Impressions," was complete. We know that *Sense and Sensibility*, once called "Elinor and Marianne," was first composed in Letters, and must therefore have been entirely re-written.

Altogether they must have been a busy six years;

though, of course, many writers have produced a larger output in a similar period. But there was hard work behind everything she did, for which the evidence, though fragmentary, is absolutely conclusive. For her the evening of life was, indeed, a fulfilling of all she had dreamed and known; putting in order the fair house of her mind and her imaginings; a wondrous legacy of fine art.

I do not believe she was unaware of the value of her own work; though utterly modest in every reference and never allowing it to obtrude within the duties of social life or interfere with family affection. On the art of fiction she is unhesitating and emphatic.

" I will not adopt that ungenerous and impolitic custom, so common with novel-writers, of degrading by their contemptuous censure, the very performances to the number of which they are themselves adding ; joining with their greatest enemies in bestowing the harshest epithets on such works, and scarcely ever permitting them to be read by their own heroine, who, if she accidentally take up a novel, is sure to turn over its pages with disgust. Alas ! if the heroine of one novel be not patronised by the heroine of another, from whom can she expect protection and regard ? I cannot approve it. Let us leave it to the Reviewers to abuse such effusions of fancy at their leisure, and over every new novel to talk in threadbare strains of the trash with which the press now groans. Let us not desert one another : we are an injured body. Although our productions have afforded more extensive and unaffected pleasure than any other literary corporation in the world, no species of composition had been so much decried. From pride, ignorance, or fashion, our foes are almost as many as our readers; and while the abilities of the nine-hundredth abridger of the *History of England*, or of the man who collects and publishes in a volume some dozen lines of Milton, Pope, and Prior, with a paper from the *Spectator*, and a chapter from Sterne, are eulogised by a thousand pens, there seems almost a general wish of decrying the capacity and undervaluing the labour of the novelist, and of slighting performances which have only genius, wit, and taste to recommend them. ' I am no novel reader; I seldom look into novels; do not imagine that *I* often read novels; it is really very well for a novel.' Such is the common cant. ' And what are you reading Miss —— ? ' ' Oh ! it is only a novel ! ' replies the young lady; while she lays down her book with an affected indifference, or momentary shame. ' It is only *Cecilia*, or *Camilla*, or *Belinda* '; or, in short, only some work in which the greatest powers of the mind are displayed, in which the most thorough knowledge of human nature, the happiest delineation of its varieties, the liveliest effusions of wit and humour, are conveyed to the world in the best chosen language."

Fanny Burney had noticed, a little earlier, that, "in the Republic of Letters, there is no member of such inferior rank, or who is so much disdained by his brethren of the quill, as the humble novelist;" and Robert Bage wrote, in his *Hemsprong*:—"Novels are now pretty generally considered as the lowest of all human productions."

Yet Henry Tilney, a man of culture and a clergyman, has said that "the person, be it gentleman or lady, who has not pleasure in a good novel, must be intolerably stupid."

Catherine had been "ashamed of liking *Udolpho*. But I really thought young men despised novels amazingly."

"It is *amazingly*," cried Henry, "it may well suggest amazement if they do, for they read nearly as many as women. I, myself, have read hundreds and hundreds. Do not imagine that you can cope with me in a knowledge of Julias and Louisas. If we proceed to particulars, and engage in a never-ceasing enquiry of 'Have you read this?' and 'Have you read that?' I shall soon leave you as far behind me as—what shall I say?—as far as your friend Emily herself left poor Valancourt when she went with her aunt into Italy."

As to the works of Mrs Radcliffe, he had read them all, "and most of them with pleasure. *The Mysteries of Udolpho*, when I had once began it, I could not lay it down again. I remember finishing it in two days, my hair standing on end the whole time."

It was the intolerable John Thorpe who had "something else to do than read novels, the stupidest things in creation, full of nonsense and stuff"; and dismissed *Camilla* as "the horridest nonsense you can imagine; there is nothing in the world in it but an old man's playing see-saw and learning Latin; upon my soul, there is not."

We may be sure that whatever Thorpe says was designed to express the thoughts of fools; while Mary Bennet and Robert Martin, remember, read *Elegant Extracts*.

At thirty-six Jane Austen was "very well satisfied" to be called "a pleasing-looking young woman—that must do; one cannot pretend to anything better now; thankful to have it continued a little longer." Whether constitutionally frail or worn out—as I sometimes suspect—by the suppressed intensity of her creative industry, she was physically enfeebled—though without any hint of a dulled mind or heart—almost before she attained maturity in years; and there were probably signs, unadmitted and possibly unobserved, of failing and fatigue; before those so painfully frequent during the last few months. Even then we find neither complaint nor depression: the book was not put aside.

Only in winter she hopes for "nice, unwholesome, unseasonable, relaxing, close, muggy weather," that she could "enjoy all over her from top to toe, from right to left, longitudinally, perpendicularly, diagonally." She has to "live upstairs and be cuddled," since "a weak body must excuse weak nerves"; until she has "nursed herself up into as beautiful a state as she can."

Cassandra suppressed many of the letters and we cannot therefore be sure of facts. But it does certainly appear as if no one realised the really serious causes of her "fever and indifferent nights" until the very last. Then her sister became "the tender, watchful, indefatigable nurse. As to what I owe to her, and to the anxious affection of all my beloved family, on this occasion, I can only cry over it, and pray God to bless them more and more."

She had been taken to Winchester, for the best available medical advice, and Mr Lyford "said he would cure her." Once more the spirit of laughter peeps out. "If he fails," wrote the dying woman, "I shall draw up a memorial and lay it before the Dean and Chapter, and have no doubt of redress from that pious, learned, and disinterested body."

Of the end, 17th July 1817, we have Cassandra's simple record.

During the last two days, "she was more asleep than awake. Her looks altered and she fell away, but I perceived no material diminution of strength, and, though I was then hopeless of a recovery, I had no suspicion how rapidly my loss was approaching. . . . She felt herself to be dying about half an hour before she became tranquil and apparently unconscious. During that half-hour was her struggle, poor soul! She said she could not tell us what she suffered, though she complained of little fixed pain. When I asked her if there was anything she wanted, her answer was she wanted nothing but death. . . . She was in a state of quiet insensibility by seven o'clock at the latest. From that time till half-past four, when she ceased to breathe, she scarcely moved a limb. . . . A slight motion of the head with every breath remained till almost the last. . . . I was able to close her eyes myself. . . . There was nothing convulsed which gave the idea of pain in her look; on the contrary, but for the continual motion of the head, she gave one the idea of a beautiful statue, and even now, in her coffin, there is such a sweet, serene air over her countenance as is quite pleasant to contemplate. . . . She was the sun of my life, the gilder of every pleasure, the soother of every sorrow; I had not a thought concealed from her, and it is as if I had lost a part of myself."

CHAPTER VIII

ROMANCE

"If you please, no reference to examples in books. Men have had every advantage of us in telling their own story. Education has been theirs in so much higher a degree ; the pen has been in their hands. I will not allow books to prove anything."

The words are Anne Elliot's, but the voice is Jane Austen's. The most reserved of all English writers did occasionally speak almost directly to us in *Persuasion*; and this appeal, from books to life, came from the speaker's heart. It is a part, moreover, of the most intimate and most moving plea for sympathy and tenderness to women, the one clear statement ever made by Miss Austen, of how well she knew the tragedy of difference between the sexes, that lurks in love. It states the claim, despite Miss Burney's triumph still far from universally admitted, that women had not only the right to be heard but a duty to speak, which is behind all her work and the measure of her achievement. It was not her way to abuse or despise men; but in many a casual allusion or chance word, she exposes the limits of their understanding, reveals the clearer insight of her own sex.

As novelist, above all, she completed the revelation of woman's mind and thought.

She would not allow "books to prove anything"; because, in some measure since mostly written by men, they were not true to life. That was the impulse of her art, to write romances of real life, true fictions, realistic tales: carrying on the work of the great fathers of the modern novel, in the light of her woman's finer instincts, intuitions, and perceptions.

Eighteenth century realism had not been, primarily, concerned to expose truth and create documents, to deny beauty and idealism, supplant painting by photograph, and enforce judgment on material evidence.

In a sense, the reformers were more interested in books than in men; at least books were their business. "In reality," said Fielding, "true nature is as difficult to be met with in authors, as the Bayonne ham, or Bologna sausage, is to be found in the shops. . . . The provision then that we have here made, is no other than human nature."

His aim was to provide a finer entertainment ; Richardson's was to insinuate a higher morality; but they were working, as craftsmen, to the same end by the same method; against "the pomp and parade, the improbable and the marvellous," which Scott himself called the "monsters" of romance.

The little printer set out to "introduce a new species of writing that might tend to promote the cause of religion and virtue": for like the author of the *Pursuit of*

Literature he had observed that, though all his young friends were "ingenious ladies, yet they are too frequently whining and frisking in novels, till our girls' heads turn wild with impossible adventures." Fielding apologises for "mere human nature," as, perhaps, "too vulgar and common," but what else, after all, is the alleged "subject of all the romances, novels, plays, and poems with which the stalls abound?"

It was, finally, Miss Burney who gave human nature to "that distinguished part of the fair sex called heroines"; discarding the "follies and nonsense, the whims and inconsistences," which had hitherto disgraced that "evergreen tree of diabolical knowledge," the circulating library.

"To draw characters from nature, and to mark the manners of the times, is the attempted plan of the following letters"; was her modest claim; and from henceforth it was not only permitted respectable maidens to read novels, but acknowledged that women could write them, without loss of virtue.

Hannah More had also noticed that in novels "nothing ever happens in a natural way":—

" It was all about my Lord, and Sir Harry, and the Captain. But their talk was no more like that of my old landlord, who was a lord, you know, nor the captain of our fencibles, *than chalk is like cheese*. I was fairly taken in at first . . . for there was a deal about hope and despair, and death, and heaven, and angels, and torments, and everlasting happiness. But when I got a little on, I found there was no meaning in all these words, *or if any, it was a bad meaning.* Eternal misery, perhaps, only meant a moment's disappointment about a bit of a letter ; and everlasting happiness meant two people talking nonsense together for five minutes. In short, *I never met with such a pack of lies.* The people talk such wild gibberish as no folks in their sober senses ever did talk ; and the things that happen ! . . . They grow rich by the stroke of a wand, and poor by the magic of a word ; the disinherited orphan of this hour is the overgrown heir of the next ; now a bride and bridegroom turn out to be a brother and sister, and the brother and sister prove to be no relations at all. . . . And except here and there one whom they make worse than Satan himself, every man and woman's child of them are all wise, and witty, and generous, and rich, and handsome, and genteel, and all to the last degree. Nobody is middling . . . like my live acquaintance, but it is all up to the skies or down to the dirt."

I do not know any more lively description of all that the old romances were, of all that Miss Austen's novels were not.

"Women in general," said Hazlitt, "have a quicker perception of character than men," and, though condemning it as a fault, he recognises that Fanny Burney "always looks at persons and things with a consciousness of her sex, and in that point of view in which it is the particular business of women to observe them."

The first serious appreciation of Jane Austen (1815), so appropriately the work of Scott, includes a most instructive comparison between the "former rules of the novel and a class of fiction which has arisen almost in our times"; unexpectedly placing *Peregrine Pickle* and

Tom Jones in the "old school"; dating the new style only "fifteen or twenty years" back.

Her contemporaries were, after all, aware of her influence upon the progress of fiction; and "the general estimate" has never gone back, since their "measured applause" began.

We can detect her aim from the regular novels; but it is only since the various irresponsible burlesques and fragmentary experiments of childhood have been made public, that we have been able to establish the zeal and thoroughness with which the harvest was prepared.

The official *Life* mentions two "effusions of fancy by a very young lady," of which *The Mystery* was "as complete as any of its kind"; and *Kitty, or the Bower* "possessed merit beyond any novel already published, or any that will ever in future appear." The "Plan of a Novel," drawn up as late as 1816, proves that she never faltered in her enjoyment of second-rate fictions, or ceased to sharpen her wit upon their extravagancies and distortions.

Here the "faultless, perfectly good and highly accomplished" heroine, and her father "the most excellent man that can be imagined," are to "converse in long speeches, and a tone of high serious sentiment." These delightful companions are never to stay "above a fortnight together in one place." She is "often carried away by the anti-hero, and now and then starved to death"; but, in the end, "crawls back towards her former country and the arms of the hero," who is, "all perfection of course." Her father is "of a very literary turn, nobody's enemy but his own"; and "after four or five hours of tender advice, expires in a fine burst of literary enthusiasm, intermingled with invectives against holders of tithes."

There will be "a striking variety of adventures," all over the world, but "no mixture" of characters. All the good will be unexceptionable, and "the wicked will be completely depraved and infamous," with "*hardly a resemblance of humanity left in them.*"

Yet as evidence of her method, and for our eternal delight, even these fascinating hints and sketches pale to trifling insignificance before the imperishable sheaf of priceless nonsense, which is *Love and Friendship*. I would not for one moment suggest that any knowledge of early Victorian novels or any critical acumen is required, or desirable, for the full enjoyment of this "clever collection of curious comments" by Miss Cooper's "comical cousin." We should as soon look up the poems parodied by *Alice in Wonderland*, before laughing with the White Knight, as count the number of fainting fits in *Santa Sebastiano* by Kitty Cuthbertson, before chuckling over the swoons of Laura and Sophia.

Yet the intimate knowledge of contemporary fiction, the close paraphrase, ornate wording, swift characterisation, and wild emotion is not only astounding in a girl of seventeen, but a foretaste, it is impossible to doubt, of her matured, subtler, methods of working on conventional romance.

How far "Sensibility" had died out in real life we cannot, perhaps, quite accurately determine. Scott and Whately, in reviewing Jane Austen, frankly lament its decay, not only in fiction but among their young friends; who, they tell us, were *not* addicted to the sacrifice of all for love:—Miss Austen's "*dramatis personnæ* conduct themselves upon the motives and principles which the readers may recognise as ruling their own and that of most of their acquaintances."

Sterne, however, "could never see or talk to the incomparable Mrs Draper without bursting into tears"; and it was his favourite boast "to have torn his whole frame into pieces by his feelings." As Yorick, he declares that, "if he could not do better he would fasten his affections upon some sweet myrtle, or seek some melancholy cypress to connect himself to."

Fanny and Susan Burney reveal in their own lives and letters, the refined tremors and heart-burnings of their favoutire heroines; and Henry Mackenzie's *Man of Feeling* was avowedly written to illustrate " the nicer and finer sensibilities of the human race." His hero discovers beauty,—"in a blush, a phrase of affability to an inferior, a tear at a moving tale." He died from shock, when the Scotch maiden "of pensive face and mild hazel eyes, confessed she could return his love":—"He seized her hand—a languid colour reddened his cheek, a smile brightened faintly in his eye. As he gazed on her, it grew dim, it fixed, it closed. He sighed and fell back on his seat. Miss Walton screamed at the sight. His aunt and the servants rushed into the room. They found them lying motionless together. His physician happened to call at that instant. Every art was tried to recover them —with Miss Walton they succeeded, but Harley was gone for ever."

These unfortunate beings could no more bear great joy than grief or alarm. Evelina was as completely prostrated by the exquisite delight of discovering a brother and being forgiven by a father, as Cecilia was disordered out of all reason by the awful tragedies she barely survived. Sarah Fielding records the sad fate of a young person who "fell from one fainting fit to another and lived but three days"—because her father forgave her.

One might have supposed that the deep and delicate emotions of sensibility would need a prolonged period of growing intimacy to mature; but this was not so. Everything in romance must be done in a hurry and the perceptions of amiable youth were instinctive, immediate, and breathlessly eager. There is, as it happens, a remark in *The Female Quixote* of Charlotte Lennox, which expounds the matter with a startling precision, worthy of Jane herself:—"*A thought strikes me, let us swear an eternal friendship.*"

Among the chief characteristics of romance-persons, we notice their strangely variegated and mixed descent, frequently "natural"; which makes their *un*-mixed characters the more surprising. The hero of Mrs Hayward's *Betsy Thoughtless* was "descended from the ancient Britons by the father's side, and by the mother's

from the Oldcastles of Kent." Since, moreover, the
charm of mystery was added unto those "whose mothers
could neither of them exactly ascertain who were our
fathers," the totally unexpected discovery of lost or
unknown relatives was a favourite device for exciting
the most passionate or pathetic convulsions:—"But
tell me, tell me, have I any other grandchildren in the
house?"

"The cruel persecutions of obstinate fathers," and a
restless disposition, drives our young people continually
from place to place; and "though tolerable proficients
in geography," they always lose their way beside a
brook or upon the mountains. The risks of the road
were, at that time, an important consideration in real
life, and we need not regard Harriet Byron's abduction
or Evelina's adventure in the Dark Walks as fanciful or
even exaggerated. Here Romance only doubled the
frequency and trebled the excitement.

This was familiar ground to Jane Austen; not for her
we imagine particularly stimulating to the emotions;
but an endless source of delight, because entirely foreign
to real life, and so deliciously absurd. That was all that
interested her at the moment. There was no one's feelings
to be hurt by the most wicked caricature: the temptation
to burlesque was irresistible. Her family and friends, we
see, were all in the game: for the complete title-novel is
inscribed to Madame la Comtesse de Feuillade; the 'trifling and unfinished' *Lesley Castle* is dedicated to Henry
Thomas Austen, Esq., drawing a kind response: "*Messrs.*

Demand & Co.—please pay Jane Austen spinster the sum of one hundred guineas on account of your Humble Servant, H. T. Austen"; the "partial, prejudiced, and ignorant" *History of England*, with "very few dates," is offered "with all due respect" to Miss Austen, eldest daughter of the Rev. George," who had supplied the illustrations; the *Collection of Letters* is Commended, with Caution and Care to her charming cousin Miss Cooper; and one of the concluding *Scraps* "On the Conduct of Young Women" is addressed on paper to her niece, Fanny Catherine; whose education had unfortunately "devolved on her Father and Mother."

We do not know, whether these ingenious satires *were* "carefully culled, collected, and classed" by their youthful author: in other words, whether they were conceived in any way, as a whole, to ridicule "Library" novelists; *or* were thrown out at odd moments when the mood took her, with no other mutual association than might arise from their being written in one notebook. It happens, nevertheless, that each supplements the other in comment upon an almost forgotten fiction form. Everything here, except the History, is in the letter-form, first adopted, as we are told, for *Sense and Sensibility* and retained in *Lady Susan*.

Love and Friendship, itself, is a complete tale of Laura's "misfortunes and adventures":—"My father was a native of Ireland and an inhabitant of Wales; my mother was the natural daughter of a Scotch peer by an Italian opera girl—I was born in Spain and received my educa-

7

tion at a convent in France." Having married the "dear and amiable Edward" at sight, she "exchanged vows of mutual friendship for the rest of our lives" with "Sophia the wife of her husband's friend, Augustus"—who "would have blushed at the idea of paying his debts," after exhausting "a considerable sum of money which he had gracefully purloined from his unworthy father." The "beautiful" young man, however, was arrested, and the adventures began. As their carriage entered Holborn, Laura "enquired of every decent-looking person that we passed if they had seen my Edward? But as we drove too rapidly to allow them to answer my repeated enquiries, I gained little, or indeed no, information." On the way to Scotland their journey is interrupted by the "horrid spectacle of two gentlemen most elegantly attired, but weltering in their blood—they were our husbands!" Edward "instantly fetching a deep sigh, expired." For an hour and a quarter Sophia "continued fainting every moment": "for two hours, not in the least fatigued," Laura "continued wildly exclaiming, 'Give me a violin. . . . Beware ye gentle nymphs of Cupid's thunderbolts, avoid the piercing shafts of Jupiter. . . . I see a leg of mutton. . . . They told me Edward was not dead, but they deceived me—they took him for a cucumber.'" In a few days, Sophia was carried off by a galloping consumption in a White Cottage; and Laura "took up her residence in a romantic village," to "indulge uninterrupted in unceasing lamentations."

This tragical outline of "confusion, despair, and pre-

cipitation," is filled in by many faintings "alternately
on sofas" or "in the open air," and complete biographies
of various friends, relatives, and acquaintances. Of these
we may mention the talented Gustavus and Philander,

" sons of the two youngest daughters which Lord St Clair had
by Laurina, an Italian opera girl. Our mothers could neither
of them exactly ascertain who were our fathers, though it is
generally believed that Philander is the son of one Philip Jones,
a bricklayer, and that my father was Gregory Staves, a stay-
maker of Edinburgh. This is, however, of little consequence,
for as our mothers were certainly never married to either of
them, it reflects no dishonour on our blood, which is of a most
ancient and unpolluted kind."

In the 13th letter Sophia had been "impertinently interrupted" while "majestically removing a bank-note"
from the private drawer of a friend; but the "excess of
sensibility" which led St Clair's grandsons, at the age of
15, to "take nine hundred pounds from their mothers
and run away" 'was more successful.' When "happily
disencumbered from the weight of so much money, they
began to think of returning to their mothers, but,
accidentally hearing that they were both starved to death,"
joined a "strolling company of players."

Lesley Castle, though nearly as long as *Love and Friendship*, is not only unfinished but uneventful: one fact
possibly accounts for the other. Jane Austen may
well have concluded it rather poor sport to further
multiply this somewhat cattish correspondence between
rival beauties and their confidantes; while a verbal

quotation from the earlier tale is more suggestive of fatigue than intention.

"No sooner did I first behold him," wrote Laura, "than I felt that on him the happiness or misery of my future life must depend." Margaret Lesley declares that "from the first moment I beheld him, I was certain that on him depended the future happiness of my life."

There is, however, an engaging description of "the innocent Louisa, sweetly smiling in a gentle nap. The dear creature is just turned of two years old: as handsome as tho' 2 and 20, as sensible as tho' 2 and 30, as prudent as tho' 2 and 40"—such is the right heroine precocity.

Sensibility in a male is hit off with equal shrewdness:— "His heart was as delicate, as sweet, and as tender as a whipt-syllabub. In a few days he was falling in love, shortly after actually fell, and before he had known her a month, he had married her."

The Collection of Letters is not, of course, a direct burlesque of fiction; being rather a compact diversion on several subjects from the illustrated "Cabinets," Elegant Extracts, or other fancy-literature of the day. Such subjects as "getting out" daughters; young ladies "crossed in love," "very much in love," or "rather impertinent" are here discussed; and we notice that tender hearts in distress are "infinitely diverted and entertained" by sad tales of another's woe ; "when one is unhappy nothing is so delightful to one's sensations as to hear of equal misery." The "superior merit" of lovers "with beautiful hair" is elsewhere remarked, for "it is no disgrace to love a handsome man," and, indeed, Musgrove's "pattern love-letter," almost outshines Mr Martin's. We applaud his virulence against Uncles and Aunts, and the laws of England,—for allowing them to possess their estates when wanted by their nephews and nieces.

Though even more detached and apparently casual than the "collected" letters, there are at least two passages, unsurpassed elsewhere, in the final "Scraps." Miss Austen has planted many a shrewd hit upon the touring habit, but once read we can never forget the "drawings of the country," taken by Fanny Johnson, "which are very beautiful, tho' perhaps not such exact resemblances as might be wished, from their being taken as she ran along beside her mother's poney."

And buried here, on almost the last page among these mere "Scraps," is written the conclusion of the whole matter; the final verdict upon "errors committed by feelings too strong for judgment":—The Confession of a Young Lady of Feeling.

"I murdered my father at a very early period of my life, I have since murdered my mother, and I am now going to murder my sister. I have changed my religion so often that at present I have not an idea of any left. I have been a perjured witness .in every public trial for these last twelve years; and I have forged my own will. In short, there is scarcely a crime that I have not committed. But I am now going to reform. Colonel Martin of the Horse Guards has paid his addresses to me, and we are to be married in a few days. He is the second son of the late Sir John who died immensely rich, . . . and took it into his head to determine on getting the whole of his eldest brother's estate. A new will was forged and the Colonel produced it in Court—but nobody would swear to its being the right will except himself, and he had sworn so much that nobody believed him. At that moment I happened to be passing by the door of the Court, and was beckoned in by the Judge, who told the Colonel that I was a lady ready to witness anything for the cause of justice, and advised him to apply to me. In short the affair was soon adjusted. The Colonel and I swore to its being the right will, and his brother has been obliged to resign all his ill-gotten wealth. The Colonel in gratitude waited on me the next day with an offer of his hand. I am now going to murder my sister. Yours ever, Anna Parker."

Miss Parker, I suspect, was comparatively mature. Maybe, in youth, she was—more conventionally—such a heroine as Laura herself:—

"Lovely as I was, the graces of my person were the least of my perfections. Of every accomplishment accustomary to my sex, I was mistress. In my mind every virtue that could adorn it was centred; it was the *rendezvous* of every good quality and of every noble sentiment."

It is improbable, I think, that any serious idea or intention lurked behind these sparkling tabloids of wit. Only just because they were written for fun, we can learn so much from them of Jane herself. The almost boisterous gaiety of phrase and thought, as Mr Chesterton has noted, "betrays her secret, which is that she was naturally exuberant. And her power came, as all power comes, from the control and direction of exuberance. But there is the presence and pressure of that vitality behind her thousand trivialities. She could have been extravagant if she liked. She was the very reverse of a starched and starved spinster. She could have been a buffoon like the wife of Bath if she chose. This is what gives a stunning weight to her understatements. At the back of this artist also, counted as passionless, there was passion; but her original passion was a sort of joyous scorn and a fighting spirit against all that she regarded as morbid and lax and poisonlessly silly."

We need no longer fear or suspect that Jane Austen's was fundamentally a quiet soul, in some mysterious way smaller than her art because content with the surface of life and men. We can now reconcile her strength with her smoothness, her intensity with her poise. Spontaneously she lashed out at folly, with every conceivable extravagance of phrase, in a storm of wit.

But she contrived to eliminate every spark of reality from the persons of her tale; the cynicism is unmeasured, and without remorse. There is no hint or effort of understanding; no mercy for the dressed dolls of literary sawdust, plunged hither and thither in torture or ecstasy by the stings of her cunning brain.

How nearly, nevertheless, they resemble the foolish originals, how interested and book-learned the author is hereby revealed, only a close familiarity with the novels of the period can fully disclose. She assumes equal knowledge and similar tastes in her own folk, for whom alone these fragments were composed, to whom no explanation

or apology was required. They prove that she grew up
and lived among books and the love of books.

With the same mastery of technique as in the published
novels, she plunges right into her subject, characters, and
atmosphere, fully confident that her readers will at once
appreciate and understand. We can feel how often they
must have chuckled with unreserved delight, as they read
of beautiful maidens with the blood of every race in their
veins; who "alternately fainted" on sofas always conveniently at hand; or who, meditating among the nettles
beside the murmuring brook, ran mad every moment for
an hour and a quarter. Novels *were* written in those
days to record "the determined perseverance of disagreeable lovers and the cruel persecutions of obstinate
fathers"; to applaud those gallant and heroic young
men, of whom it could never be said that they had obliged
a parent.

It would be easy, of course, to say in our haste, that
such pitiless severity only proves that Jane Austen was,
after all, cynical at heart, mercenary or conventional in
her moral outlook, prosaic in her instinct of common
sense. In the exuberance of youthful parody, there is,
indeed, obvious cynicism—naked and unashamed. We
see here a sparkling epitome of *inhuman* romance, which
is the coldest and most material selfishness; a picture of
reckless idleness and enjoyment, as the meaning of
marriage. We find unmeasured scorn for the callous
absurdities of so-called generous youth. But the appli-
cation throughout is to dramatic sawdust. It is a

criticism, and reproduction, of art, not of life; of the heroine who "at eighteen was angelic, for she had a smooth white skin and £12,000."

The complete change of tone, the new note—of reality *and* tenderness (speaking her love of man in *serious* criticism of false romance)—is obvious from the first in the regular novels.

I believe nevertheless that she *left in* a few romance-persons, or types (lifted from the old novels without the Austen touch); to whom she remained cynical and almost mercilessly cold.

Such character-parts as Lady Catherine and Mr Collins should be compared with Mr Woodhouse and Miss Bates. The former are exaggerated without fear, lashed without mercy. Their absurdities are more extreme and more mechanically consistent than would be possible in real life. She had no feeling for or about them, nor have we. Lady Catherine was, in a way, intellectual, but she was not remade by the emotions, and we scarcely think of her as a woman.

There is a hint for Mr Collins in Sarah Fielding's *David Simple*, where the gentleman kindly expounds "the whole duty" of wives:—

"I shall expect nothing of you but that you will retire into the country with me and take care of my family. I must inform you that I shall desire to have everything in order, for I love good eating and drinking, and have been used to have my own humour from my youth; which, if you will observe and comply with, I shall take care of the main chance for you and your children."

Mr Woodhouse may be a trifle overdone; Miss Bates, perhaps, is laboured beyond human nature. Yet both are handled with an unmistakable tenderness that endears them to all. There was no one to care for Lady Catherine, as Emma loved her father; no one to respect Mr Collins as we all respect Miss Bates. The clergyman cared for no one, as the old maid loved her mother.

Miss Austen did not do much for the Thorpes, General Tilney, or Mrs Palmer. Lady Middleton she afterwards humanised in Lady Bertram.

But the most significant example of fiction-types is surely Lydia Bennet. We have all, I suspect, been a little uneasy about the whole episode of her disgrace. Elizabeth's thoughts turn almost immediately to what effect her sister's "infamy must produce" upon her "own noble suitor." Even Jane sorrowed little for Lydia herself; and Darcy's generous "patching-up of the disgraceful affair" lacks the human sympathy of Colonel Brandon for the unfortunate Eliza, though *his* responsibility towards mother and daughter recalls Mr Villar's anxious care for two generations.

Miss Austen's ruthlessness towards Lydia, her crisp, placid dismissal of the crude flirt, can only be willingly accepted as an almost casual use of the typical "frail female" of fiction: a distasteful being to whom she has not actually given life; for whom, therefore, she feels no moral responsibility. Towards Maria she is equally severe, but with genuine moral passion: towards Eliza she is forgiving: while the similar perils which Marianne

Dashwood and Georgianna Darcy only narrowly escaped, prompt her to pitying love.

It is towards Lydia, and Lydia only, that Miss Austen can fairly be charged, by thoughtful readers, with moral conventionality or a hard heart. She can only be justified or understood, if we look on Lydia as fiction-made, not emotionally created: a mere "borrowed" tool to scaffold the plot.

Of *Love and Friendship* itself Jane Austen made very little use, far less than of the unfinished *Watsons*. She did, however, revive a large number of the names, not only Charlotte, Marianne, and Maria; but Annesley, Musgrove, Cleveland, Crawford, Dashwood, and Willoughby.

Mr Chesterton detects "something like the first faint line in the figure of Fanny Price" about the "girl in the white cottage," who "was nothing more than a mere good-tempered, civil and obliging young woman; as such we could scarcely dislike her—she was only an object of contempt." He hears the unmistakable voice of Mr Bennet, in the "aggravating leisure and lucidity" with which the heroine's father "enquires the nature of the noise, when a loud knocking is heard on the outward door of the Rustic Cot":—

" It certainly does appear " (said my father) " to proceed from some uncommon violence exerted against our unoffending door." " Yes " (exclaimed I), " I cannot help thinking it must be somebody who knocks for admittance."

" That is another point " (replied he) : " we must not

pretend to determine on what motive the person may knock—
tho' that someone *does* rap at the door, I am partly convinced."

Many readers must have agreed with Elinor that Mrs
Dashwood's "generosity was overstrained" by her
delicate "refusal to force the confidence" of a daughter.
In the same spirit, however, when Sophia was longing to
"learn the fate of her Augustus—to know if he is still in
Newgate or if he is yet hung," she could only cry to
Heaven for information:—"Never shall I be able so far to
conquer my tender sensibility as to enquire after him."

These parallels in phrase or thought are little more
than conjectures, on somewhat flimsy foundations. But
the "abominable rudeness" of Miss de Burgh in "keeping
Charlotte out of doors in all this wind" was very probably
adapted from Lady Greville's insulting consolations to
poor Maria, who "was obliged to stand" beside her lady-
ship's carriage "though the wind was extremely high and
very cold."

" It is a horrible east wind. . . . I assure you I can hardly
bear the window down. But you are used to being blown
about by the wind, Miss Maria, and that is what has made
your complexion so ruddy and coarse. You young ladies who
cannot often ride in a carriage, never mind what weather you
trudge in, or how the wind shows your legs. I would not have
my girls stand out of doors as you do in such a day as this. But
some sort of people have no feelings either of cold or delicacy."

The passage occurs in the "third" letter of the "collection," which is, in fact, a full and remarkably lifelike
sketch-study for Lady Catherine's ordinary conversation,

her impertinent curiosity, and her genius for mortifying the young.

But *Love and Friendship* does not approach Miss Austen's idea of work or art. Not so would she speak to the world: and with very good reason. In the first place it is intellectual without heart. There is not one glimpse of human nature, one touch of life. The splendid vivacity of burlesque never animates the Romance novel, the inhuman humanity of the writers she has so gaily exposed. There are names, but no people; there is wild melodrama, but no plot. The irony is reckless, cynical, and hard. In writing for her friends there was no need to champion humanity. They knew her heart and their own hearts. For them she could lash out at literature without the risk of being misunderstood. It was the stupid public who would add flesh and blood to Laurentina's skeleton; and mistake Counts in Italy for real men.

Yet the way is prepared. The foundation is here. With the same criticism differently expressed, the novels were no less certainly created from books, correcting the false pictures of romance, changing the *in*human *dramatis personnæ* to living human beings.

Was it chance or foresight that inspired the startling sentence "from Laura to Marianne," in which the atmosphere of every novel is painted in eleven words?

"Our neighbourhood was small, for it consisted only of your mother."

CHAPTER IX

AN EXPERIMENT

"What could I do? Facts are such horrid things."

It may be that no more significant reason than its inconvenient length determined the long withholding of *Lady Susan* from the public view.

It was, however, a youthful experiment, written we learn between *Love and Friendship* and the first novel, possibly with no thought of publication. It is, like those enchanting "Scraps," a manifest imitation of early fiction, on entirely different lines from any of the novels offered for print, and equally merciless in its calm, cynical irony. It is, on the whole, therefore most probable that Miss Austen would have refused to publish, even if desired, so cold a picture, above all of a woman and a mother.

Suggestions have been put forward that this so-called unfinished sketch might have been filled in with a firmer hand to "put things in proper proportions." But though the correspondence is discontinued, with apparent abruptness, "to the great detriment of the Post Office revenue," and a "Conclusion" provided in narrative form ; I see no reason to suppose that Jane Austen ever contemplated elaborating the final episodes of the story, or that any such re-writing is required to reveal the characters or do justice to their charm. The work seems to me admirably finished and complete.

It is, moreover, of peculiar interest to the critic, because of its striking dissimilarity from Miss Austen's usual mood—only in one respect resembling even *Love and Friendship*; and because it belongs to the small school of picaresque fiction, seldom practised in England, but including such acknowledged masterpieces as Defoe's underworld tales, *Count Fathom*, *Jonathan Wild*, and *Barry Lyndon*.

In this type of novel the villain must dominate the entire plot, as this accomplished coquette most assuredly does; and Lady Susan injures, in some degree, literally everyone in the book. She secures the reader's interest throughout, and it is on her that Miss Austen has devoted her most careful work. The art is studied and deliberate, almost mature; never yielding to dash or abandon. She entirely avoids (again thus discriminating from *Love and Friendship*) the sordid material of criminal adventure (not scorned by Thackeray), which is the recognised foundation of ordinary picaresque work. But the heroine is vicious to the core, though only once betraying herself perfectly ready and willing to commit murder provided she could never be found out. The confidante, Mrs Johnson, is given more than a hint in the following words:—

" Mainwaring is more devoted to me than ever ; and were we at liberty, I doubt if I could resist even matrimony offered by *him*. This event, if his wife live with you, it may be in your power to hasten. The violence of feelings, which must wear her

out, may be easily kept in irritation. I rely on your friendship
for this."

The field of Lady Susan's chief criminal activities, the
scene of her daily occupation, the stimulus to her
pleasure, is the happy home, which she can "rob of its
peace in return for the hospitality with which she was
received into it." She "does not confine herself to that
sort of honest flirtation, which satisfies most people, but
aspires to the more delicious gratification of making a
whole family miserable."

She easily conducts three or four dangerous affairs at
the same time, satisfying all, giving herself to none;
though, at the time the story opens, nothing was going
smoothly "with the females of the family united against
her," and she was thus driven to comparative retirement
in that "unsupportable spot, a country village," at the
home of a conveniently wealthy brother-in-law, who
"lived only to do whatever he was desired."

Even here difficulties arise, chiefly through her
attempts to bully her daughter Frederica, whose "feelings are tolerably acute. She is so charmingly artless
in their display as to afford the most reasonable hope
of her being ridiculous, and despised by every man
who sees her." The child had run away from a school
in Wigmore Street, where the "price is immense and
much beyond what I could ever attempt to pay";
and, in the end, proves to be her mother's most dangerous rival; detaching her from the very man whose
fortune she had decided to marry.

The complexities, purposes, and achievements of this woman without a heart are recorded, with Miss Austen's matured mastery of wit, in a series of letters, in which a hundred slight touches and chance words reveal her astounding insincerity, ingenious effrontery, and the brilliance of her superficial attractions; incidentally opposed by the equally designing but less able Miss Mainwaring, "who, coming to town, and putting herself to an expense in clothes which impoverished her for two years, on purpose to secure him, was defrauded of her due, by a woman ten years older than herself."

For "though one would not suppose her more than five and twenty," she was, in fact, unmistakably middle-aged: yet "an excessively pretty woman, delicately fair, with fine grey eyes and dark eyelashes."

"One is apt, I believe, to connect assurance of manner with coquetry, and to expect that an impudent address will naturally attend an impudent mind; at least, I myself was prepared for an improper degree of confidence in Lady Susan; but her countenance is absolutely sweet, her voice and manner winningly mild . . . yet what is this but deceit ? "

She is not, however, quite clever enough to be a success. She subdued men but could seldom hold them; and on no occasion does she conquer the "circumstances"; which were, for her, other women.

It is a very short book, containing few characters and practically no events, yet we are startled, on reflection, at its unsparing revelations of the incalculable amount of mischief that may be done by sheer empty-headedness, entirely without strong feeling or passion; and of the incredible isolation in which such a character must always live.

She has not a friend in the world. Insomuch as never for one instant does a single thought for anyone but herself cross her mind, so never does anyone else show one spark of affection for her; outside her many lovers, who only desire her for their pleasure.

The cutting prophecy for her future, which closes the narrative, is in Miss Austen's best manner. She had been driven to marry, for an establishment, the complete fool she had designed for her daughter:—

"Whether Lady Susan was or was not happy in her second choice, I do not see how it can ever be ascertained; for who would take her assurance of it on either side of the question? The world must judge from probabilities; she had nothing against her but her husband, and her conscience."

There is internal evidence that for whatever reason, Miss Austen had quite determined against publication, if ever contemplated; for she repeats the episode of Frederika's running away in *Pride and Prejudice*, and only slightly varies a judgment upon the constancy of men, for reissue in *Mansfield Park*. The hero, young de Courcy, had been absolutely infatuated by Lady Susan, and only permanently disillusioned in Letter **XXXIV**.

" Frederika was now fixed in the family of her uncle and aunt, till such time as Reginald could be talked, flattered and finessed into an affection for her ; which allowing leisure for the conquest of his attachment to her mother, for his adjuring all future attachments, and detesting the sex, might be reasonably looked for in the course of a twelvemonth. Three months might have done it in general, but Reginald's feelings were no less lasting than lively."

In the case of Edmund Bertram:—

" I purposely abstain from dates, that everyone may be at liberty to fix their own, aware that the cure of unconquerable passions, and the transfer of unchanging attachments, must vary much as to time, in different people. I only entreat everybody to believe that exactly at the time when it was quite natural that it should be so, and not a week earlier, Edmund did cease to care about Miss Crawford, and become as anxious to marry Fanny as Fanny herself could desire."

Marianne required two years to conquer her devotion to Willoughby in favour of Colonel Brandon.

CHAPTER X

THE FIRST THREE

"It is a new circumstance in romance, I acknowledge, and dreadfully derogatory of a heroine's dignity ; but if it be as new in common life, the credit of a wild imagination will at least be all my own."

This is, of course, one of the most frankly daring lies ever ventured in print. Jane Austen knew, and assumed that her readers would at once perceive, that her delicate disclosures of Catherine's heart were copied direct from *Evelina*. That young person gave herself away to Mr Villars the moment her eyes fell on Lord Orville, and, unless the women were unbelievably slow at detecting a "partiality," all her friends must have seen the state of her heart. In actual fact this new circumstance in romance is as old as Adam in real life, though in fiction, perhaps, originated by Sam Richardson; with far less delicacy or feminine intuition. He studied females, however, with greater daring than Fielding; and what was conventional in Pamela was, after all, courageous in Harriet Byron. She decided upon Sir Charles, many long chapters before that estimable man made up his mind to leave Clementina. The mother of Miss Burney's *Camilla* expressed the orthodox view, when she rejoiced in the virtuous delicacy of her daughter, that "so properly, *till it was called for*, concealed her tenderness from the object who so deservingly inspired it"; and Mrs Opie informs us that her Adelaine's "feelings of delicacy were too strong to allow her to sigh for a man who evidently had no thoughts of sighing for her."

But Jane Austen's adaptations from Fanny Burney cover a wide ground. She was steeped in novels from childhood, often merely amused and delighted, occasionally stirred to enthusiasm and generous praise. Always alive to the enterprise and superiority of her own sex—for whom she spoke at times with most vigorous resolution; her deepest loyalties and affection were concentrated upon the author of *Camilla*.

There is little decided priority among the novels of the first group, but all three are built round parody or imitation—not as in *Love and Friendship*, of fiction-types, but specifically of Mrs Radcliffe and, more intimately, of Fanny Burney. Every critic must find occasion, it seems, of comparing Jane Austen with Will Shakespeare; and certainly she approaches him in her supreme indifference to comment when lifting plot, character, or theme.

Like all young people she began writing to exercise her wit, more interested in books than mankind, though always alert to correct romance from real life. The later group are less book-built, more humane, and—in one view—more original or independent.

The three first novels are at the same time more auto-

biographical than the second. She *uses* herself and
Cassandra, as sisters, an alliance afterwards more
artistically constructed between Emma and Harriet
Smith, where contrast of taste and temperament are
better justified by distinctions of birth. Elinor and
Marianne, in their different ways, regret leaving Norland
Park, as Anne more subtly lives in the past, and Jane
Austen herself is said to have fainted on suddenly hearing
that her father had decided to give up Steventon. I
have already suggested that Catherine Morland's childhood was quite directly borrowed from Jane's. But
these personal details belong to the mechanism of the
plot, later varied or abandoned for more artistic construction, built for the characters of the piece.

The serious, or fundamental, parts of *Pride and Prejudice*, *Northanger Abbey*, *Sense and Sensibility* come from
books.

Marianne, perhaps, is nearer to Fanny Burney than to
Evelina. But she was invented to win our affection, if
not our respect, for that literary refinement of elegant
females called *Sensibility*, which distinguished the two
younger Burney sisters among the robuster Bohemians of
their day; as it at once delights and provokes us in her
youthful heroines,—above all, *Camilla*. There is not a
hint of cynicism in Marianne Dashwood.

But if the concluding sentence of *Cecilia* determined
both title and plot of *Pride and Prejudice*; the last words
of *Camilla* point no less directly to *Sense and Sensibility*.

" Thus ended the long conflicts, doubts, suspenses, and sufferings of Edgar and Camilla ; who, without one inevitable calamity, one unavoidable distress, so nearly fell the sacrifice to the two extremes of IMPRUDENCE AND SUSPICION, to the natural heedlessness of youth unguided, or to the acquired distrust of experience that had been wounded."

Now that "happy little person" "Camilla" has not only greater sensibility, but more charm than "Evelina" :—

" Every look was a smile, every step was a spring, every thought was a hope, every feeling was joy. . . . Her disposition was ardent in sincerity, her mind untainted with evil. The reigning and radical defect of her character—an imagination that submitted no control—proved not any antidote against her attractions : it caught, by its force and fire, the quick-kindling admiration of the lively ; it possessed, by magnetic persuasion, the witchery to create sympathy in the most serious."

Could words, more truly or more eloquently, paint Marianne Dashwood? The punctilious Edgar is carried away by "the utmost vivacity of sentiment, all the charm of soul, eternally beaming in the eyes, playing in every feature, glowing in the complexion, and brightening every smile."

For Edgar Mandlebert, though his natural caution had been unfortunately nursed into suspicion by a tutor whom women had twice deceived, stands, like Elinor, for "Sense." He, too, is older than his years; more than once forced, by circumstances, to adopt an air of wisdom and to undertake practical responsibilities, scarcely becoming to youth; but at heart equally tender, generous, and forgiving; with affections no less deep and sincere.

The contrast is here used to produce misunderstanding, naturally so between lovers; but it remains the foundation of the plot, as in *Sense and Sensibility*. It was, we can scarcely doubt, the "origin" of Miss Austen's tale.

The deplorable Johnsonese of Miss Burney's later style, and the Bedlam-melodrama of the concluding chapters, which are even wilder than those of *Cecilia*, have buried *Camilla* in an early grave, from which, I fear, there is no awakening. But could one retell the story, with some omissions, in its author's earlier manner, I believe it would prove to be her most popular work.

The characters are strongly individual: Eugenia, "dear little Greek and Latin"; that "most exquisite workmanship of nature," Indiana Lynmere; that "sad fellow" Lionel; and the wicked Clermont; the wily Miss Margland and the naïve Sir Hugh.

Miss Austen, at any rate, appreciated its worth. Her name appears in the "list of subscribers," she couples it *with Cecilia* in her well-known spirited defence of novels; she encourages John Thorpe's sneers at its "horrid nonsense," therefore proving her own admiration.

The characteristic of Sensibility is so foreign to Jane herself, so obviously not present in any member of her family; that it can only, I think, have been chosen from romance—and what other romance could have served her purpose so well, or so naturally have come to mind, as *Camilla* ?

Because, however, she was no less aware of its absurdities than of its charm; she permits some humour, and some moral condemnation, in her treatment of Marianne; but she is far more sympathetic than critical, an attitude that was derived from her interest in an earlier type of girl she could only have known from books, only loved or appreciated, as drawn by Fanny Burney. It is, moreover, a justification of the grace, from which she has deliberately cut out those exasperating passion-storms in which Evelina indulges towards her long lost, and almost entirely unworthy, father; and which Cecilia exhibits to even further extremity in the tiresome closing chapters of her almost maniacal distress. These, we note, were not present in Fanny Burney herself. They serve, meanwhile, to disgust many readers, though not apparently of her own generation, with any and all such characters whatsoever. Jane Austen freely caricatured them in *Love and Friendship*, more subtly in Isabella Thorpe. Here she reveals their innate charm.

There is a clear distinction between true and false sensibility, which Jane probably recalled, in Mrs Radcliffe.

" Do not, my dear Emily," said St Aubert, " indulge in the pride of fine feeling, the romantic error of amiable minds. Those who really possess sensibility ought early to be taught that it is a dangerous quality, which is continually extracting the excess of misery or delight from every surrounding circumstance. . . . We become the victim of our feelings, unless we can in some degree command them . . . for happiness arises in a state of peace, not of tumult ; it is of a temperate and uniform nature ; and can no more exist in a heart that is continually alive to minute circumstances, than one that is dead to feeling.

" You see, my dear, that, though I would guard you against the dangers of sensibility, I am not an advocate for apathy. At your age I should have said *that* is a vice more hateful than all the errors of sensibility, and I say so still. . . .

" Beware, my love, I conjure you, of that self-delusion which has been fatal to the peace of many persons—beware of priding yourself on the gracefulness of sensibility ; if you yield to this vanity, your happiness is lost for ever. . . . Do not, however, confound fortitude with apathy, apathy cannot know virtue."

The heart of every heroine of the old romance was "formed for violent and lasting attachments only." Isabella carried "her notions of friendship pretty high," and made friends at first sight; Sophia and Laura "instantly unfolded to each other the most inward secrets of our hearts."

In *Love and Friendship* a more serious aspect of the indulgence of "Sensibility" up to middle-age is revealed: a striking comment upon the real virtue of Mrs Dashwood. The lady here, as age will, is recalling her lost youth:—"A sensibility too tremblingly alive to every affliction of my friends, my acquaintance, and particularly to every affliction of my own, was my only fault, if fault it could be called. Alas! how altered now! Tho' indeed my own misfortunes do not make less impression on me than they ever did, *yet now I never feel for those of another*."

Yet does not Anne's instinctive and reasoned preference for the daring ardour of Captain Wentworth, stand to prove that Miss Austen, too, held apathy a more "hateful vice"; one that "cannot know the virtue of fortitude."

In Marianne, and almost more delightfully in Mrs Dashwood, we see the real delicacy of feeling, the sensitive refinement of taste, the responsiveness to fine shades; which made Fanny Burney and Evelina better "ladies" than most of their friends and acquaintance, of Bohemia or the *tons*; and in some ways, more modern. They had, unfortunately, however, that self-delusion fatal to many of *priding* themselves on their gracefulness. They *yielded* to this vanity, and their happiness was lost—"though not for ever."

Elinor speaks for Jane Austen; loving their childlike enthusiasm and warm hearts, while tenderly lamenting their selfishness and their folly. A more careful and critical picture of the conventions of romance, it would be hard to conceive. It is not drawn from life, but from books—corrected from human nature. Only here, at least, Miss Austen would have us remember that, for all their generous, but dangerous, absurdities, their virtues were greater than their faults.

For when Marianne's eyes were opened to Elinor's real strength of affection and a suffering far deeper than her own, she still blushed for that sister's calmness, but "of the strength," and depth, "of her own feelings she gave a very striking proof by loving and respecting that sister." In fact she really loved Elinor and her mother more than Willoughby. She "could never love by halves," even a "gentleman who sought the constitutional safeguard of a flannel waistcoat"; but she "overcame an affection formed so late in life as at seventeen";

she "submitted to new attachments" and learned to "find her own happiness in forming her husband's."

As Jane Austen attributes Catherine's love for Henry to "wild imagination"; she describes Marianne's as "an extraordinary fate," because she knew that both were the natural and proper cures of disappointment. She has reconciled Fanny Burney to real life.

Turning now to *Pride and Prejudice*, we meet Miss Burney again, more specifically in character and situation, less obviously, perhaps, in taste and sentiment. The very title and all the machinery of the plot is here lifted from *Cecilia*; with an affectionate admiration that gave no thought to possible criticism lying in wait for the plagiarist. In the earlier novel, a long, and at times a wearisome, series of accidents and misunderstandings is encouraged to separate the destined hero and heroine from the happiness they are so perfectly fitted to enjoy. "The whole of this unfortunate business," remarks their best friend, "has been the result of PRIDE AND PRE-JUDICE."

"First Impressions," as it had been originally called, was already completed. Certainly Darcy was the embodiment of Pride; certainly Elizabeth had been Prejudiced against him from the first. Like Delvile and Cecilia they were long divided by these very facts. The stately Darcy, too, had fallen in love against his will: the offence of his hesitating proposals, though not due to a foolish Will, was dictated by similar emotion no less unbecoming a gentleman or a lover. Both young men discoursed at length upon their struggles between pride and passion to the young ladies they desired to honour with their affection. Both resisted long, yielded in the end, and were forgiven.

Elizabeth again, like Cecilia, understood better, as she knew more of, the temperament and the obligations natural to noble birth and family conventions. She learned to respect the sense of honour and inherited uprightness, that had at first presented themselves to her as both absurd and intolerable.

Both tales are primarily controlled by sharp antagonisms and gradually softening estimates, towards complete understanding between the two. The outstanding scenes in each novel, though one in no way imitates the other, run on closely parallel lines.

Darcy, like Delvile, is "not more eloquent on the subject of tenderness than of pride." He has, indeed, overcome his scruples and offers his hand, in confidence of its being accepted, to one who dislikes and despises him. Delvile, on the other hand, wishes merely to explain the reasons that have induced him to deny himself the dangerous solace of the society of one whom he believes entirely indifferent to him, and to excuse the occasional outbursts of tenderness into which he had been betrayed at unguarded moments.

He does not complain of "the inferiority of her connections," but of the clause in her uncle's Will by which her future husband·is compelled to relinquish his own name for hers.

Cecilia had been puzzled by his uncertain behaviour, but, believing him only cautious from respect to his parents, had permitted herself to love him. She had not Elizabeth's sense of personal injury to support her annoyance; or any convictions of his haughty injustice to others.

Jane Austen, indeed, has created a more dramatic situation; because the quarrel is based on fundamental antipathies between the lovers themselves; but little affected by a͞   ͞istracting considerations of family influence to ͞   ͞ "shameless avowal of his abominable pride."   not mince her words:—

"͞   ͞ Darcy, if you suppose that ͞   ͞ affected me in any other ͞   concern which I might ͞   ͞ behaved in a more gen͞   ͞ot have made me the o͞   ͞le way that would have tem͞   ͞rom the very beginning —from the   may almost say—of my acquaintance w͞. ͞ ͞our manners, impressing me with the fullest belie͞ ͞ of your arrogance, your conceit, and your selfish disdain of the feelings of others, were such as to form that groundwork of disapprobation on which succeeding events have built so immovable a dislike."

There had been nothing in Delvile's conduct, to her or to others, that could have drawn such indignation from Cecilia. Her misery—and his,—because due to almost fanciful and perversely strained emotions on either side, was both less natural in them and less moving to us. One scene almost irritates: the other entirely delights.

Between Mrs Delvile and Lady Catherine, the differences are even more fundamental. The mother, like the aunt, based her appeal on the "honour and credit" of the young man she was so anxious to release; but her insolence was tempered by affection, and disguised by high-sounding moral sentiments. She came to appeal, not to scold. And Cecilia was softened, as most assuredly Elizabeth had never been, by a sense of gratitude for past kindness and by a strained notion of respect—not *altogether* undeserved.

Miss Austen everywhere discards melodrama or the assistance of violent emotions to pile up the agony. She has used the machinery of a plot based on accidental and largely unreasonable difficulties; to construct one built from character and the inevitable inconveniences of an attachment between young people so differently brought up. The morbid tears of a Delvile are abandoned for a gay laugh at a de Burgh. Life replaces the stage.

On the surface *Northanger Abbey* more closely resembles *Love and Friendship*; and seems altogether more experimental than any other of the novels. It is primarily an exposure or laughing caricature of romance types and the machinery of fiction. As I believe also the Morlands are most intimately sketched, as a group, from the Austens; and Henry's utterly charming manner of awakening Catherine's mind and improving her knowledge, is surely a loving tribute to her own elder brothers, no less tender because drawn with swifter wit than the paternal loving-kindness of Edmund Bertram.

Again, the obvious incidents and conversations from Mrs Radcliffe, her *Mysteries of Udolpho*, occupy a great part of the canvas. Catherine Morland not only devours these fascinating "Horrid Mysteries" with the naïvest enthusiasm; but applies their unnatural pictures of life to an interpretation of her own experience, which we can only forgive for its delicious absurdity. The instantaneously inspired eternal friendship with Isabella Thorpe at once transports us away from real life to false romance; and when the thrill of entering an abbey and gazing upon an "ebony cabinet" so "conspicuously situated" in her bedchamber, has stimulated the heroine's fevered imagination, we are ready to face "the pine forests and the vices" of the Pyrenees, the fiends and the "spotless angels" behind the "black veil"; to forget "that we are English—that we are Christians."

Catherine is not afraid for herself: "the courage" of a heroine "did not fail her"; but she proceeds to harbour and elaborate the most wild suspicions of her highly respectable and aristocratic host, which, when ultimately confessed, draw from Henry a gentle but unqualified expostulation against "the influence of that sort of reading which she had indulged" in Bath; disclosing the moral and critical purpose of Miss Austen's gay caricature, the inspiration of all her art. It was not, perhaps, "in the charming works of Mrs Radcliffe and all her imitators, that human nature was to be looked for."

Yet more subtly and—as it were—beneath the surface, *Northanger Abbey* is largely derived from Fanny Burney; in a general situation and type of character which Miss Austen never made use of again.

The full title of Miss Burney's first novel was *Evelina*; or, *The History of a Young Lady's Entrance into the World*; and the author modestly wrote in her Diary that she "has not pretended to show the world what it actually *is*, but what it *appears* to a young girl of seventeen."

Catherine Morland is not only equally deficient in knowledge and worldly wisdom: she too is suddenly launched into a very mixed society from a sheltered clerical home, with no useful advice from her simple-minded guardians; while Mrs Allen, like the Mirvans, forgot—if she ever knew how—to warn her against young men or tell her the rules at balls and assemblies. The Thorpes are little better than the Branghtons, though less formally "no class," and, in their somewhat crude characterisation, might have been drawn by Fanny Burney herself. John had "benefited" no more from the University than Mr Collins, and though his gallantry does not resemble Mr Smith's in form, it is objectionable for the same reason.

But towards the fascinating Tilney, Catherine becomes Evelina herself. It is not only that she at once perceives him to be the most wonderful and charming man in the

9

world; not only that she immediately places her fluttering heart in his, without a moment's pause to wonder
if he had given a thought to her. There are in both girls
the same subtly superior refinement and real delicacy of
mind—which is the secret alike of Evelina's charm and
Miss Burney's—something a little different, which lends
grace to their tiresome innocence and folly: preparing
us for unsuspected moral strength and deep feeling, to
capture at last our unqualified admiration in the quiet
and dignified tact of Catherine's cruelly hurried departure
from the Abbey.

It is Henry of course who develops her character
and mind; precisely as Orville looked after Evelina's:
in both cases without the aid of any older woman. This
is the theme and foundation of both tales. The extraordinary advance upon anything in Fielding or Richardson, achieved by the true chivalry, delicacy, and innate
good breeding of Lord Orville;—his surprising tact and
daring comradeship towards Evelina—modern despite
its stilted phrase and courtly bow—has seldom, if ever,
received the praise it deserves.

We do not look for subtlety in Miss Burney; it was
her business to reveal women; and we are rather inclined
to question the licence she seems always ready to give
"the gentlemen" of her world.

But Jane Austen appreciated and understood. I would
almost say that Tilney is a finer gentleman than Darcy:
he can unfold a maiden's heart, direct her thoughts, and
stimulate her intelligence, with a lighter touch and more

understanding sympathy than Knightley or Edmund Bertram.

Though none of the second group are thus worked out on suggestion from Miss Burney or other novelists; they contain characters or situations which remind us, as they were no doubt intended, of something in *Evelina* or *Cecilia*.

The pompous Mr Delvile reappeared altogether in General Tilney, and gave an air to Sir Walter Elliot. Cecilia could never determine "whether Mr Delvile's haughtiness or his condescension humbled her most," and he became "at length so infinitely condescending, with intention to give her courage, that he totally depressed her with mortification and chagrin." Catherine Morland always found that "in spite of General Tilney's great civilities to her, in spite of his thanks, invitations and compliments, it had been a release to get away from him."

Emma's imprudent friendship with Harriet Smith is essential to the plot. But in developing it, Miss Austen can scarcely have failed to welcome the chance of once more following and—as it were—affectionately touching up Miss Burney. For Cecilia, too, was for ever watching the state of Henrietta's heart; and though too wise to attempt directing her affections, was now soliciting her confidence and again, from motives of prudence, rejecting it. For a time, both girls were in love with the hero, and Henrietta dreamt as fondly and foolishly over Delvile's imagined partiality as Harriet did over

Knightley's. Miss Austen, moreover, explains what Miss Burney assumed, that the heroine has never a thought of resigning her lover to her friend, or of "resolving to refuse him at once and for ever, without vouchsafing any motive, because he could not marry them both."

Other verbal recollections occur again and again.

Miss Steele's persistence in laughing at herself about "the doctor," and Tom Bertram's affected belief that Miss Crawford was "quizzing him and Miss Andrews," are both of a like mind with Miss Larolles when Gosport reports the rumour thàt "she had left off talking."

" Oh, was that all," cried she, disappointed. " I thought it had been something about Mr Sawyer, for I declare I have been plagued so about him, I am quite sick of his name."

" And for my part, I never heard it ! So fear nothing from me on his account."

" Lord, Mr Gosport, how can you say so ! I am sure you must know about the festino that night, for it was all over the town in a moment."

" What festino ? "

" Well, only conceive how provoking ! Why, I know nothing else was talked of for a month."

When Anne Elliot moved to the end of a form at the concert, to avoid missing Captain Wentworth, "she could not do so without comparing herself with Miss Larolles, the inimitable Miss Larolles, but still she did it, and not with much happier effect."

The "voluble" lady, for her part, had been determined to catch the *ennuyé*, Mr Meadows:—

"Do you know he has not spoke one word to me all the evening! though I am sure he saw me, for *I sat at the outside on purpose* to speak to a person or two that I knew would be strolling about; for if one sits on the inside there's no speaking to a creature you know; so I never do it at the opera, nor in the boxes at Ranelagh, nor anywhere. It's the shockingest thing you can conceive, to be made to sit in the middle of these forms, one might as well be at home, for nobody can speak to one."

We have often noticed the self-centred masculine futility of Edmund's attempt to comfort his dear cousin:—"No wonder—you must feel it—you must suffer. How a man who had once loved, could desert you. But yours—your regard was new compared with—Fanny, *think of me.*"

So when "the best of men," Mr Villars, is penetrated to the heart at sight of Evelina's mortal distress, he can only exclaim: "I cannot bear to see thy tears; for *my* sake dry them: such a sight is too much for me: *think of that*, Evelina, and take comfort, I pray thee."

It was the same reverend gentleman who taught the amazing Mary to draw a moral from a sister's shame. For he once bade dear Evelina to remember that "nothing is so delicate as *the reputation of a woman; it is at once the most beautiful and most brittle* of all human things."

So Mary remarked:—

"Unhappy as the event must be for Lydia, we may draw from it this useful lesson: that loss of virtue in a female is

irretrievable—that one false step involves her in endless ruin—
that her reputation is no less brittle than it is beautiful, and that
she cannot be too guarded in her behaviour towards the un-
deserving of the other sex."

Emma's wicked suspicions of Miss Fairfax were encouraged, if not excused, by the unselfish kindness of
her employers. "The affection of the whole family, the
warm attachment of Miss Campbell in particular, was
the more honourable to each party, from the circumstance of Jane's decided superiority, both in beauty
and acquirements."

Evelina similarly put Miss Mirvan entirely in the
shade, but no suspicion of jealousy ever clouded their
affection, and Mrs Mirvan was no less generous and kind.

There are hints to be found from Madame D'Arblay's
Camilla and the more deservedly forgotten *The Wanderer.*

Miss Margland's conduct towards Sir Hugh Tyrold
and his adopted children has in it something of Mrs
Norris; Mr Westwyn's naïve enthusiasm for his own son
resembles Mr Weston's. The prevalent idea of female
culture observed and scoffed at by the unfortunate
Wanderer is thus epitomised in *Camilla*:—"A little music,
a little drawing, and a little dancing, which should all
be *but slightly pursued,* to distinguish a lady of fashion
from an artist."

We remember Miss Bingley's claims for an accomplished woman, who "must have a *thorough* knowledge
of music, singing, drawing, dancing, and the modern

languages." Lady Susan, indeed, knew the world far better:—

"Not that I am an advocate for the prevailing fashion of acquiring *a perfect knowledge* of all languages, arts, and sciences. It is throwing away time to be mistress of French, Italian, and German ; music, singing, and dancing. . . . I do not mean, therefore, that Frederica's acquirements *should be more than superficial*, and I flatter myself that she will not remain long enough at school *to understand anything thoroughly.*"

"A lady," as Mr Delvile informs us, "whether so called from birth, or only from fortune, should never degrade herself by being put on a level with writers, and such sort of persons."

Such borrowings cast no reflection upon Jane Austen's originality, and should not tempt us to criticism. They establish our conviction of her intimate familiarity with the fictions she always loved and sometimes laughed at: they convince us of her profound loyalty to the pioneer sister-novelist; they prove that, with equal zeal if less pretension than the masters of an earlier generation, she was determined to correct romance from real life.

The three first novels, all her work at Steventon, were more or less deliberate adaptations of *Camilla*, *Cecilia*, and *Evelina*; certainly based on the characters and plots of these novels, and inspired by her enthusiasm for them.

CHAPTER XI

THE SECOND THREE

Consideration and esteem as surely follow command of language as admiration waits on beauty, and here I have opportunity enough for the exercise of my talent, as the chief of my time is spent in conversation.

There are no further adaptations in the second group —*Mansfield Park*, *Emma*, and *Persuasion*. She may, indeed, have come to regard such methods as a little immature. It may simply have been that having, as it were, exhausted Miss Burney, she was necessarily dependent upon her own invention for atmosphere, characters, and plot.

Emma, indeed, has always been coupled with *Pride and Prejudice*, mainly because comparison between the heroines is inevitable; but there is no fundamental similarity outside the writer's strong personality and individual style. None of the six, in fact, is so conspicuously free from the class mixture always used by Miss Burney, on which the tale of Darcy and Elizabeth altogether depends.

The comedy parts are here more human and less caricatured, better fitted into the plot. Miss Bates and the Eltons are absolutely at home in Highbury. Emma has more character and less wit than Elizabeth. Her faults towards Harriet, Miss Bates, and Frank Churchill produce more completeness of personality, a more individual human being; perhaps the most fully developed of all the heroines: at once more domineering, sillier, and more emotionally "converted" when she discovers herself. Because Harriet is not her sister, but very differently born and bred, the contrast of character needs no excuse: being rather inevitable, what must have existed and everyone would expect. She is naturally independent as an only child, the cause at once of her weakness and her strength.

Again the under—or secondary—plot of Jane Fairfax and Frank Churchill demands greater skill in construction than Miss Austen ever attempted elsewhere. In fact the advance in technique is obvious and considerable; and though still without adventure or deep emotion, the scene and movement are varied and full. Nothing more natural, and in another sense more subtle, could have been devised to temper Emma's somewhat unpleasing arrogance and tendency to domineer, than her exceptionally sincere and wholly spontaneous affection for a most tiresome parent; which, moreover, gains for him our respect. Because she is never impatient with him, never permits herself the least suggestion of a smile at his fads, we are at least as much impressed by his courtly manner and kindly feeling for all the world, as by the delicious absurdity of his gruel and his childish objection to draughts. He is, after all, conspicuously a gentleman in the best sense of the word, tenderly proud of his daughter and genial to his friends: something very much bigger than a mere figure of fun. In a different way, Miss Bates is lifted above her absurdities by respect, despite Emma's cynical estimate of the world's contempt for a poor spinster. Darcy, I think, would not have played the gentleman so well as Knightley with Miss Bates; though very possibly had he, too, appeared among his own people, we should never have heard the suggestion that Miss Austen did not quite know what good manners required from a man.

Jane Bennet's persistence in thinking everyone good and pleasant is occasionally exasperating, tempting one to call her insipid. Jane Austen is very far from any-thing of the kind; but she has the gift of seeing and revealing strength and charm in the most unpromising material. Obviously humour helps; but it is not only the laughter they arouse which secures our affection for Mr Woodhouse and Miss Bates: not felt, you should observe, for the Eltons, Lady Catherine, or Mr Collins; because they are mean in heart, the one quality for which there is no touch of mercy in Miss Austen's con-tempt. She does not crush the vulgarity of Uncle Phillips as she stamps on "Mrs E."

The inspiration of her humour is not cynical; how-ever bold and broad the human parody may be, it does not distort or caricature in spite. Where the wit directs us to hate or unmeasured derision, it is not from its cruelty, but from the moral ugliness of its subject.

In these later novels, I do not find any of the romance-persons left in from type and the cold intellectual wit of the critic has no place here; transformed to a discriminating charity for mankind.

All the change we can detect in the maturity of Miss Austen's work is derived from development in technique, more practised construction, and the greater intensity of her affections: mind and heart strengthening together, with the years; the exuberance of youth scarcely diminished. The form of the work, in atmosphere and subject, remains the same; the personality behind it has no new desires or ambition. She is still working within the small circle of the folk she knew and loved, still writing novels such as had been the joy of all her life and, assuredly, had not lost their savour. She does not dive into the storms of passion that may tear up our lives, which, in her judgment, do not concern the novelist. She had hated them in the false frenzy of romance. Her ideal is still reform, not revolution; the perfecting of her chosen domain, not the adventure into new realms of primitive or exotic man.

How benevolent is the Knightley-Woodhouse sovereignty over their well-ordered and cheerful little world; most precisely defined, perhaps, by Emma's very honest confession of annoyance at being denied the dignity of "refusing" an invitation from the worthy Coles. Doubt has been thrown on her descent from gentility to wound Miss Bates; and it was certainly not becoming a lady. But Mrs Elton's vulgarity could not fail to prove occasionally infectious; and though Emma herself was not aware of the fact, Miss Austen certainly intends to show us that her manners and good feelings suffered a little deterioration when wilfully playing up to Frank Churchill's dishonourable double-dealing. Nothing more clearly indicates Miss Austen's serious moral principles than her stern reproof of this irrepressible young man, whose dash and high spirits she could no more resist than Emma herself. Outspoken rebuke was left, with subtle artistry, to his jealous rival, who could not repress his just indignation.

Frank Churchill cannot appear in Highbury, from the great world, without disturbing its serene existence. Only a fashionable young man, accustomed to society, could have ventured upon the delightful absurdity of going to London to have his hair cut, or secretly presenting a piano to the lady of his choice. And it is he who most appropriately exhibits Miss Austen's admitted taste for flirtation, to which Emma so happily responds. In examining her own feelings towards the gay deceiver, Miss Woodhouse has borrowed a little from Miss Austen's half-serious letters about Tom Lefroy.

Frank's philandering is less spontaneous than Henry Tilney's or Captain Wentworth's; partly, of course, from the necessity for disguise, but more fundamentally because his nature and breeding had been more worldly-wise. Like Jane Austen, he could have given "lessons" in the art to his simple friends.

The Fairfax mystery is Miss Austen's one experiment

in intrigue, at times threatening to develop a sex tri-
angle. But that was not her way. She knew from the
first that Emma's feelings would not be involved,
though her pride was hurt and her vanity offended.
Miss Woodhouse was to be gently fooled, for edification;
not wounded or heart-broken. It is a merrier, and
more ingenious, device for disturbing the course of
true love, than the sad tale of Elizabeth's undesirable
connections.

The worldly element once introduced was apparently
recognised by Miss Austen as a valuable asset. It is
more pronounced in *Mansfield Park*, where social contrasts are revived and carried to greater extremes; so
furiously condemned by Mrs Norris as "the folly and
nonsense of people's stepping out of their rank and
trying to appear above themselves." The Crawfords
are more sophisticated than Frank Churchill and more
degenerate; Mrs Price "married, in the common phrase,
to disoblige her family, and by fixing on a lieutenant of
the marines, without education, fortune, or connections,
did it very thoroughly." The step up, through Mrs
Norris, to the lucky sister Maria, who "captivated Sir
Thomas, with only seven thousand pounds," is far
steeper and affords more opportunity for farce than the
gradual descent from Mr Bennet to Uncle Phillips through
Mr Gardiner, so respectably in trade. I wonder if Miss
Austen was tempted, for once, to so crude a mixture of
manners by affectionate recollections of the romances she
had ridiculed in her youth. The situation of Fanny Price

certainly approaches the old way for heroines, seldom the way of life. She is forcibly removed, by the plot, from where she belonged, to prove herself heroic; with that surprising innate superiority to her mother and sisters, which was a favourite device of the romance-writers, always oblivious to nature or probability. Susan was not destined to be a heroine; and therefore achieves more practical advantage from the change. Unhampered by delicacy or refinement she slips easily into Fanny's place, rather intent upon the material luxuries of Mansfield Park than any romantic ideal of marrying the prince. Her virtues are solid and commonplace. They have their reward.

The Bertrams, in fact, may almost be said to achieve adventure. Awakened thus, in two contrary directions, their placid and stately County residence is somewhat rudely invaded. Actual drama is used as Miss Austen never again employed it. The Crawfords could never have been really at home for long at Mansfield Park, as Tom Bertram, in one glorious moment of suppressed laughter, was allowed to perceive:—

"His father's looks of solemnity and amazement on this, *his first appearance on any stage*, and the gradual metamorphosis of the impassioned Baron Wildenheim into the well-bred and easy Mr Yates, making his bow and apology to Sir Thomas Bertram, was such an exhibition, such a piece of true acting, as he would not have lost upon any account. It would be the last —in all probability—the last scene on that stage; but he was sure there could not be a finer. The house would close with the greatest éclat."

Fanny's sudden return to Portsmouth is also drawn for the stage:—"She was at home. But alas! such a home! She was almost stunned." The "trollopy-looking maid-servant," her father's "language and smell of spirits," the kicking of shins, slamming of doors, shouting of boys, must have seemed to her like some hideous nightmare of another world: a pantomime in undress, "featuring" ugliness and noise.

For once the quiet of her usual "setting" is broken up, and Miss Austen allows the devil to enter in. Henry Crawford, rather by accident, indeed, than as accomplished villain, involves himself in a moral problem the really virtuous Frank Churchill had so dexterously escaped. His double-dealing was more profound. He had "destroyed Maria's happiness," he could "not be satisfied without Fanny Price, without making a small hole in Fanny Price's heart." But heroines must be approached with caution and respect. Miss Austen must humble the gilded youth. In the end, we know, it was Fanny who captured Henry: the family dependent, the poor relation, who caught the man of the world. That was the proper climax of romance, the expected reward of innocence and humble virtue; only Miss Austen was not writing romance.

Even so I have sometimes wondered whether art or morality decreed that Henry Crawford should leave the company in disgrace. The small party of critics who give Fanny the prize in the fascinating game of preference among Miss Austen's heroines, are even prepared to

quarrel with her on this account; making the girl more
clear-sighted than her creator:—

"From several earlier indications we surmise that Crawford
might have won Fanny at last, and this is more plainly stated
towards the end of the book. . . . If so, so much the worse
for Fanny. To have transformed her affection from Edmund
to Henry, to have accepted, after so much talk of principle, a
man of Henry's easy morality, would have made her less
interesting as well as less virtuous. ' Would he have persevered
and uprightly '—in there lies the secret of the Crawfords' failure,
and I could wish Jane Austen had not lowered Fanny to the
possibility of a marriage with Henry. No; it would have been
better than this that Edmund should marry Mary and be
dragged down by her, and Fanny go on helping Lady Bertram
in her work. She had been so clear-sighted in perceiving the
want of proper feeling and sincerity in the brother and sister
that it is hard to believe she could ever have so completely
condoned it."

I admire the loyalty of this comment, without reserve.
The courage to put Jane Austen in the wrong and sacrifice Edmund with a gesture, almost persuadeth me to
believe. But I am not convinced; for the simple reason
that I, also greatly daring, would accuse Miss Austen on
another count. I believe that Crawford "*would* have
persevered and uprightly" had he been consistently
developed. And I believe the Henry Crawfords would
have been not only more agreeable and interesting, but
a finer couple, than the Edmund Bertrams. Miss Austen
was wise indeed to drop the curtain upon the deadly
dullness of that pious home.

There should, certainly, be no doubt on such a question. We are criticising Miss Austen by quarrelling about her plot. The moral issue admits of no such dispute. It was plainly necessary to punish Maria for a loveless marriage, to expose Mrs Norris and her pretended genius for managing other people's affairs, to reveal Sir Thomas as an inadequate parent, to let the evil influence of the wicked Admiral do its work.

But I suspect that Miss Austen was also influenced by a certain private obstinacy she justified by following literary conventions. Because Henry Crawford had been given the villain's part, he could not marry the heroine, and she would not modify her "plan"; even though probably aware that she was "passing" a slip in characterisation, allowing herself to risk not convincing the reader. In the first place, she had no use for villains without virtue. And in developing the better side of Henry's nature, she was caught,—as Emma had been caught by Frank Churchill's idle gallantry,—and fell a little in love with him herself. Led on insensibly to justify her own partiality, she gave him also stability of character and "moral taste," a perfectly natural change of heart. There had never been any real vice in his thoughtless selfishness, nothing a serious attachment could not naturally cure. The man who accepted Fanny's family, without a suspicion of patronage or derision, was genuinely in love; and could never have fallen to Maria Rushworth, "without even the excuse of passion." The days were long passed for such criminal folly. His

10

sister maintained to the last that Fanny "would have fixed him; she would have made him happy for ever." Surely Fanny was one to find her own happiness in making others happy.

The worldly element in *Mansfield Park*, however, was not only used for serious moral issues. It fills the picture with busy crowds. Such amusing and character-revealing episodes as the rehearsals of *Lover's Vows* enliven the domestic routine; Mr Rushworth's inanities are magnified by contrast, and the visit to Sotherton Park, to be "improved" according to Crawford, supplies an agreeable subject of conversation. One character-part, kin to Collins or Mrs Elton, remains; and Mrs Norris excellently sustains her rôle.

For several reasons, *Persuasion* stands almost entirely apart. The inevitable interest attached to a favourite author's last book is justified and strengthened by an entirely new note of deep feeling and emotional characterisation, which brings us very near the author, with almost startling effect.

Once more, the bustle of *Emma* and *Mansfield Park* has been discarded for the old quiet family scene; but gossip and fun take a back seat, used only for illustration or relief, to reveal a new and perfectly matured power for the searching analysis of human nature, that could have been reckoned supreme among a very different group of similarly inspired predecessors.

No longer than *Northanger Abbey*, it has neither the intrigue-complexity nor the crowded canvas that mark experience in others of the second group. It is written throughout in a minor key, without one outstanding comic character-part. We smile at Sir Walter Elliot, or the family of Uppercross, and applaud the swift polish of many a witty phrase; but, however subtle and permeating, the humour does not anywhere prevail over emotion.

The construction is even more compact and balanced than ever before, with a new depth, tenderness, earnest feeling. Anne does not capture the reader at sight with the brilliance of an Emma or an Elizabeth; though she is no less obviously superior to her own family, and has in reality more character. Never recognised at home, as were all Miss Austen's heroines save Fanny Price, she yet dominates the story more than any. It is even less sensational than any of its predecessors, with no animated social functions—not one ball—no figures of fun, no clash of types.

Yet in all its detail, Miss Austen uses the now familiar material of character and situation, adventures no further from the home, almost repeats herself in plot. Anne's misery and happiness alike arise, as did Jane's and Elizabeth's, from a refinement to which every other member of her family, and most of her friends, were absolutely blind. She is, spiritually, as much the only child of a foolish father as Emma Woodhouse. The natural understanding between two sisters is again disturbed by rivalry for the one eligible visitor in the neighbourhood, though happily without any consequent disaster.

Captain Wentworth wickedly pays attention to two young ladies at once, like Frank Churchill and Henry Crawford. His "intentions" are no less freely discussed. The naïvely conceived villain of the first group has become—again, as in *Mansfield Park*—an accomplished man of the world, with no sister indeed to further his perfectly honourable designs on the heroine but, in the last event, not lacking a female accomplice for more vicious ends. Its most striking effect in local colour, the glowing picture of naval types, was foreshadowed in William Price. Society, as in *Northanger Abbey*, is located at Bath; domesticity dwells, like the Dashwoods, at the Park Gates, in daily intimacy with the Squire.

Only here, at last, there is rest from the satire that had dominated Jane Austen's art from the beginning. Here we witness the final triumph of her love for man over her delight in caricature and hatred of false romance. There are no half-made, inhuman parodies of nature, temporarily holding the stage, distracting us a moment from the drama of real life. The infectious high spirits, the untamed joy in glorious nonsense, the comradely English laugh at "the dear fool that is part of every man," has completely vanished,—for the moment at least, may be for ever.

To replace our loss, Miss Austen consents at last to reveal something of her private thoughts and most sacred convictions; spoken here to open the eyes of men. Anne has been given the experience of suffering to speak for her, on

" the nature of any woman who truly loved. . . . We certainly
do not forget you so soon as you forget us. It is, perhaps,
our fate rather than our merit. We cannot help ourselves. . . .
God forbid that I should undervalue the warm and faithful
feelings of any of my fellow-creatures ! I should deserve utter
contempt if I dared to suppose that true attachment and constancy were known only by woman. No, I believe you capable
of everything great and good in your married lives. I believe
you equal to every important exertion, and to every domestic
forbearance, so long as—if I may be allowed the expression—
so long as you have an object. I mean while the woman you
love lives, and lives for you. All the privilege I claim for my
own sex (it is not a very enviable one ; you need not covet
it), is that of loving longest, when existence or when hope
is gone ! "

These are strong words, strongly spoken. Miss Austen
has conquered her reserve of feeling, her restraint of
phrase. And we must not omit to add, the fuller revelation that naturally comes with happiness restored. Anne
is not, Jane Austen was not, a woman content, or ever
desiring, to weep. She does not believe that true love is
"on the side of safety." Anne was "wrong in yielding
to persuasion." Her tragedy was her own fault. Life
had taught her, not greater caution or prudence, but more
daring and more confident hope. Were the risk to be
offered now, she would welcome it with open arms. At
the door of death, whether or no she saw it opening to
receive her, Jane Austen deliberately, clearly, and emphatically prefers the dashing impetuosity, the manly
charm and impulsive wooing of a Wentworth, over the

pleasing and courteous eloquence of an Elliot, the motherly wisdom of a Lady Russell. We have seen Anne Elliot in the early autumn of her youth, troubled with memories of what might have been, though serene and happy in a quiet corner of good deeds. But we leave her to a future of bright sunshine, of gay love. "Her spring of felicity was in the warmth of her heart. She gloried in being a sailor's wife."

CHARACTERS AND PLOTS

SENSE AND SENSIBILITY

(WRITTEN AND REVISED BETWEEN 1796 AND 1798 : PUBLISHED
1811. ORIGINALLY COMPOSED 'IN LETTERS' AS ELINOR
AND MARIANNE)

THE romantic tale of an old-world heroine, Marianne Dashwood, personifying the eighteenth-century charm of extreme " sensibility," contrasted with, and corrected by, the more modern " sense " of her sister, Elinor : a ' correction ' from life of popular fiction.

Mrs Dashwood and her three daughters (the youngest, Margaret, scarcely coming into the plot) are left in comparative poverty at her husband's death, which the appalling selfishness of her wealthy stepson, John, does nothing to relieve ; and they, accordingly, settle down in a Devonshire cottage adjoining Barton Park, residence of the genial Sir John Middleton and his stately, cold-hearted, wife. Before the tale begins Elinor had been quite clearly ' distinguished ' by Edward Ferrars, the elder brother of John's wife, Fanny (who brought him £10,000), but, though returning his love, was in her own mind, both puzzled and distressed, by his failure to propose.

This sober romance, however, is long kept in the background ; while Marianne's more vivid and uncontrolled emotions are allowed full play. At sixteen she gives her heart, without reserve, to the handsome young Willoughby, who eagerly

responds to her generous enthusiasm for books and the picturesque, with equal indifference to the common courtesies of
life or the feelings of others.

Nothing, however, is said of marriage or even an engagement ;
Willoughby suddenly leaves them without explanation ; and,
after some chapters of stormy distress, is heard of in London,
engaged to the rich Miss Grey. It ultimately appears that,
being entirely dependent upon his old cousin, the severely
moral Mrs Smith, who " dismissed him for ever " on somehow
hearing that he had seduced and abandoned a young girl, he
was driven to marry money.   Marianne is completely prostrated
for a time ; but, gradually realising her sister's brave endurance
of *her* troubles, resolves to face life once more ; and " over-
coming an affection formed so late in life as at seventeen, with
no sentiment superior to strong esteem and lively friendship,
voluntarily gives her hand " to the elderly Colonel Brandon,
who had loved her from the first.

It is now known to the reader that Edward Ferrars had been
trapped into an engagement with the vulgar Lucy Steele
(daughter of his tutor) ; and was too honourable to break it off,
though permitting himself to love, and tacitly woo, another.
When the facts are at last disclosed, however, the wily ' villainess,'
at the same time, refuses to release him *and* catches his dandified
brother Robert, who, having no character but good looks, is
readily forgiven and made his mother's heir. Thus freed, the
hero can speak, and is happily married.

All " sense " here is concentrated upon the elder girl ; as
Mrs Dashwood is no less romantic and eagerly emotional than
Marianne herself.

The interplay of the two love-stories provides a considerable
variety of scene and events ; the humorous element being further
supported by the Ferrars family, Lucy Steele and her foolish
sister, the tactless facetiousness of Sir John, and the astound-

ing vulgarities of Lady Middleton's kind-hearted, but stupid, mother and sister.

The social relations between the Middletons at the Park and the Dashwoods at the Cottage, curiously anticipate Miss Austen's own family experience in later years. The deep love between the sisters, often used in the novels, is an echo of her own feeling for Cassandra Austen.

"Sensibility" was, of course, familiar to Jane Austen from the heroines of romance; though, while revealing its absurdities and false emotional refinement, she has also captured its essential charm. We can almost imagine Marianne to have been drawn from Fanny Burney, herself a conspicuous example of *real* sensibility; while the contrast with "sense" recalls the whole atmosphere and scheme of the sister-novelist's *Camilla*, often praised by Jane Austen, which is itself constructed upon a somewhat more violent opposition of similar emotions: "the extremes of Imprudence and Suspicion." Marianne is a second Camilla. Elinor has much in common with Edgar Mandlebert.

PRIDE AND PREJUDICE

(Written 1796, 1797 : Published 1813)

The title *First Impressions* originally given in manuscript, to this novel, further defines its subject; of love begun, not indeed with a little aversion but, for the heroine at least, with most decided antipathy.

It is again the story of two sisters, or twin-heroines, Jane and Elizabeth Bennet: the eldest in a family of daughters, but infinitely superior to the rest; Mary, a vain and stupid pedant; Lydia, "a common flirt"; and Catherine, her pale echo. Mr Bennet, having early recognised the vulgar inanity of his match-making wife, disowns all responsibility for her and the younger girls, though loving the heroines ; and asks only two things of life—uninterrupted solitude among his books, and the privilege of laughing at his acquaintance.

The leading hero, Fitzwilliam Darcy, of Pemberley in Derbyshire, first appears, as visitor to the charming and simple-minded Charles Bingley (suitor and destined husband of Jane), and is immediately declared by the whole neighbourhood, to be more insufferably proud and forbidding than even his great riches can excuse. To Elizabeth his character is further privately misrepresented, by ungrateful malice, as cruel and unjust to his dependents, while the natural disdain openly expressed for her impossible relations, hardens her heart, despite an unwilling mental respect and sympathy.

When therefore love conquers pride, though not so far as to forbid its tactless and frank expression, and forces from him a condescending declaration, Elizabeth's scorn and indignation know no bounds. He cannot deny, or even regret, having detached Bingley from Jane—" towards *him* I have been kinder than to myself "—and many chapters of mutual repentance and explanation, many events revealing them more justly to each other, are needed to make them " the happiest couple in the world."

Darcy's great influence over his friend had been supported by the latter's upstart sisters ; Carlone Bingley, who wanted Darcy for herself, and the colourless Mrs Hurst. They easily persuaded his modesty of Jane's indifference, while sneering at her connections. *They* intend him to marry Darcy's sister, Georgiana. But Darcy had learned from Elizabeth, how deeply her sister's hidden feelings had been involved ; and, when ready to ' try again ' himself, he brings back the forgiving young man to his beloved.

It was George Wickham, Lieutenant in the Militia, the wicked son of Darcy's family steward, who told lies about him, while lightly flirting with Elizabeth—entirely to her delight. He had, in fact, persuaded Georgiana Darcy, when only fifteen, to an elopement, luckily cancelled by confession : when pressed for debt, he deserts Elizabeth for Miss King " with ten thousand pounds," but fails to catch her : and, in the last event, carries off the reckless and infatuated Lydia to obscure lodgings in London, with no thoughts of marriage, till bullied and generously bribed by the hero,—in true service of Love.

The whole story is enlivened by most infectious wit, in the telling thereof—with Elizabeth's gay comments ; and by the introduction of two outstanding comic types : the Right Hon. Lady Catherine de Burgh, Darcy's aunt who, on hearing of her nephew's infatuation, immediately calls on the Bennets, to compel Elizabeth to give him up : and the Rev. William Collins, pompous and servile rector to Lady Catherine, on whom the Bennets' property is entailed ; who makes a ludicrous proposal to Elizabeth, and when at last convinced of her indifference, immediately marries her mercenary friend, Charlotte Lucas.

There are full-length portraits of Elizabeth's two aunts ; the common, good-natured Mrs Phillips, and the admirable, refined, Mrs Gardiner ; and of their foolish neighbours Sir William and Lady Lucas. The scene is varied by Elizabeth's visit to Mrs Collins, introducing Lady Catherine ; and by her tour in Derbyshire with the Gardiners, giving a favourable impression of Darcy at his family estate.

This novel contains the fullest and most intimate picture of two inseparable sisters (so often drawn by Miss Austen from her love of Cassandra) ; and the plot is implicitly derived from Fanny Burney's *Cecilia*, wherein " the whole unfortunate business had been the result of Pride and Prejudice." Miss Austen has exchanged the " contrivance " of a foolish Will for natural and instinctive incompatibilities ; but Delvile hesitates even longer than Darcy, for similar reasons, and proposes with almost equal offence : his mother pleads with Cecilia to release him, affectionately indeed, but on precisely the same grounds as Lady Catherine.

The sensational emotions of romance are once more tempered by characterisation from real life. On a general view, Elizabeth's nature and conversation obviously resemble Jane Austen's.

NORTHANGER ABBEY

(WRITTEN 1797, 1798 : PUBLISHED, POSTHUMOUSLY, 1818)

THE simple love-story of Catherine, eldest daughter of the Rev. Richard Morland—of Fullerton, Wilts ; who, though born to be a heroine, leaves home for the dissipations of Bath, with no maternal warnings against " the violence of noblemen and baronets " ; and no other guide to conduct or manners than an exhortation to " wrap herself up very warm about the throat at night, and keep some account of the money she spends."

Like Fanny Burney's *Evelina*, in loving memory of whom her character and adventures seem to have been inspired, Catherine fortunately meets the hero almost directly she is launched into Society ; and, from henceforth, happily commits herself to his amused and kindly direction. Henry Tilney is also charmed at sight by her transparent sincerity (" She does not *want* to talk to anyone " else), and " the natural folly of a beautiful girl " ; gradually learning to recognise the real strength and loyalty of her affectionate nature.

The course of true love is long assisted by General Tilney's, mistaken, impression of her financial expectations (supposing her heiress to Mr Allen, with whom she had come to Bath) ; but rudely interrupted at last by the old gentleman's indignation, and outrageous incivility, on discovering the Morlands to be " a necessitous family ; numerous, too, almost beyond example . . . a forward, bragging, scheming, race."

Such " cruel persecution of an obstinate parent " naturally
stirs the hero to haughty defiance. Hurrying to Catherine's
side, he immediately begs, and wins, " that heart, which, they
pretty equally knew, was already entirely his own " ; and,
" within a twelvemonth from the first day of their meeting,
the bells rang and everybody smiled "—to see " perfect happiness
begun at the respective ages of twenty-six and eighteen."

Two subjects are introduced to colour this placid tale.
Catherine Morland, like Jane Austen herself, had " read hundreds
and hundreds of novels," acquiring thereby an " intimate knowledge of Julias and Louisas." Prepared thus for the artificial
romances of " Love and Friendship," she falls immediate victim
to the vulgar insincerities of Isabella Thorpe, already secretly
engaged to the undergraduate James Morland ; and is tormented
by the colossal conceit, and unwelcome attentions, of her
friend's brother John, a *dis*agreeable " Rattle," gaily drawn from
type like the ' Larolles ' or the ' Meadows ' of *Cecilia*. From
the crude selfishness of Miss Thorpe, and her wicked manner of
flirting with Henry's brother, the Captain, while " in love with
James," Catherine learns a little about real life, not told in
novels. John Thorpe is further skilfully woven into the plot by
being made the casual instrument of General Tilney's delusions ;
exaggerating both the Morland's wealth and their poverty.

Catherine's interest in Henry, again, is both enhanced—and
complicated, by his living in an Abbey ; from which her enthusiasm for " all Mrs Radcliffe's works," induces her to expect
the most alarming mysteries, finally worked up to wild suspicion of General Tilney, who must have murdered his wife.
Once more " the visions of romance are destroyed : most
grievously was she humbled, most bitterly did she cry." But
real life, after all, proves more wonderful than fiction ; for
Henry actually forgives " the liberty which her imagination
had dared to take with the character of his father."

Northanger Abbey, in fact, is constructed from books : the heroine and her adventure being based on *Evelina* ; the temporary infatuation for Isabella Thorpe and *her* false romantics, upon the novels burlesqued in *Love and Friendship* ; the imaginary crimes suggested by ' a visit to an abbey,' upon *The Mysteries of Udolpho*.

Henry Tilney very intimately reflects Jane Austen's own attitude towards life and humanity : his careful explanation of the need for ' correcting ' romance by observation of real life, may be accepted as a definition of her art.

MANSFIELD PARK

(Written between 1811 and 1813 : Published 1814)

The startling contrasts between members of the same family, apparently accidental in *Pride and Prejudice*, are here more naturally introduced by the varying fortunes of marriage. The beautiful Miss Maria Ward of Huntingdon, despite her absolute lack of character, having captured Sir Thomas Bertram of Mansfield Park. Miss Ward " finding herself obliged " to accept the Rev. Mr Norris, deceased before the story begins ; and Miss Frances having " very thoroughly disobliged her family " by marrying the impossible Mr Price, a lieutenant of the Marines.

The scene is set by Sir Thomas condescending to adopt his eldest niece Fanny Price, a modest and shrinking creature, accustomed to privation ; who finds herself sadly neglected and ill at ease, among her elegant cousins ; and is consistently bullied by the snobbery of her widowed aunt. Destined, however, like Catherine Morland, to be a heroine, her simple virtues, her unfailing attention to Lady Bertram's needlework and pet dogs, gradually reveal the innate superiority of her mind ; until she captures the villain's hitherto wandering heart; and—in the final chapter—the hero "becomes as anxious to marry Fanny, as Fanny herself could desire."

It is, in fact, the younger son, Edmund Bertram, who guides and comforts her from the first ; to whom, again like Catherine, she confides herself in every difficulty and distress. He is long attracted, however, by Mary Crawford, the villain's charming sister, herself more worldly than the Bertrams, disposed to scoff at the Church, and not particularly fixed in any principles of morality.

For the greater part of the story Sir Thomas is engaged on business abroad, leaving the intolerable Mrs Norris in charge. This vulgar and managing woman quickly contrives a "great" match for Maria Bertram, with the almost imbecile James Rushworth of Sotherton Court, worth £12,000 a year. The vain and selfish Maria would clearly have been quite content with this magnificent establishment ; had not Fate intervened by bringing Henry and Mary Crawford on a visit to their half-sister, the rector's wife. Henry immediately starts to flirt with both sisters at once, without serious intentions to either. Mary responds, with more feeling, but no decided affection, to Edmund's courtship; and Fanny grieves over the blindness of all her cousins to the dangers ahead.

When Sir Thomas unexpectedly returns, to most dramatically interrupt the various social frivolities his absence had made possible, Henry prudently withdraws from a compromising situation, and Maria's pride teaches her to go through with the marriage she now dreads and abhors.

This is the signal for Fanny to take the centre of the stage. Crawford idly turns his mind to "making a hole in her heart," only to find himself badly captured. Sir Thomas, naturally, approves the excellent connection for his humble charge ; and when baffled by her quiet but firm refusal, conceives the ingenious idea of sending her home again—to learn, by contrast, the advantages of wealth. It proves, indeed, a hard lesson; and Miss Austen's picture of the sordid family in Portsmouth is almost unkindly grim.

But meanwhile Henry Crawford has called on the Rushworths: piqued by Maria's pretended indifference, renews his attack on her heart; is, in his turn, miserably surprised by the passion of her response, and thus driven, by sheer frivolity and high spirits, into carrying her off. Julia Bertram, fearing parental strictness, immediately runs away with a casual, but not criminal, acquaintance; and the horrified distress at Mansfield Park may be imagined.

Completely justified by universal consent, the heroine is promptly summoned to console and support the mortified pride of her rich relatives. Edmund is most effectively disillusioned by Mary's shocking levity over her brother's sin; and " when it was quite natural that it should be so, and not a week earlier, did cease to care about her," and married his cousin.

This is Miss Austen's most complex plot : her most serious introduction of worldliness and immorality. Yet Henry's genuine culture, his real gift for reading aloud; and the vivacious descriptions of amateur theatricals are directly drawn from her own family experience.

EMMA

(WRITTEN 1814, 1815 : PUBLISHED 1816)

MORE specifically a character study than any of the earlier group, this story is based upon an entirely original plot, ' improved ' from the unfinished *Watsons*; though occasional episodes and situations still recall Fanny Burney.

It lives by gentle raillery of Miss Emma Woodhouse, undisputed mistress of her invalid father's home, and leading lady of a ' small neighbourhood,' socially inferior; where none but the manly hero, George Knightley, Squire of Donwell Abbey, ever dares to oppose her will or criticise her conduct. As his brother John had married Isabella Woodhouse before the story opens, he appears no more than a pleasant, if sometimes provoking, member of her own family ; not remotely suggesting thoughts of love till the closing chapters : the chief example of Jane Austen's theory of the ideal marriage—founded on intimate understanding.

Here the central motive or governing emotion is only seen beneath the surface : our interest and amusement being fully occupied by Emma's injudicious attempt to cultivate the silly Harriet Smith ; detaching her from honest Robert Martin, and encouraging her to admire various ' real ' gentlemen, who either scorn or ignore her ; till the great lady's willing pupil dares at last to dream of the hero himself, translating his courteous and kindly attentions, given for Emma's sake, to evidence of partiality. Whereby the heroine learns the state of her own heart.

Emma's first choice for Harriet had been the Rev. Philip Elton, an intolerable but purely comic cleric (fit comrade to Collins) who, in fact, aspires to Miss Woodhouse, but, being rejected with scorn, captures Augusta Hawkins—the vulgarest female of fiction ; and many comedy scenes are created out of these events, with ample support from the delicious absurdities of Mr Woodhouse, and the immense loquacity of Miss Bates.

Like Eliza Bennet by Wickham, Emma was first temporarily attracted, by the elegant Frank Churchill ; whose equally marked, but more refined, flirtation is actually an adroit covering for the sub-plot, of his secret engagement with the accomplished Jane Fairfax (outshining Emma at her instrument), a poor governess, visiting her aunt, Miss Bates. Towards her, Miss Woodhouse sadly forgets herself in cruel private jokes with Churchill on a supposed, improper, affection for her former pupil's Irish husband. The whole story is skilfully woven within the main plot, further exposing Emma's lack of wisdom, and providing a delightful combination of pathos, comedy, and intrigue, nowhere else attempted in the novels. Frank Churchill enters the circle as stepson of Emma's former governess, the admirable Mrs Weston.

In the foolishly romantic intimacy of Harriet and Emma, Miss Austen can hardly fail to have had in mind Cecilia's no less indiscreet attentions to Henrietta Belfield. There is no copying here of motive or incident, but Henrietta, too, humbly adored the hero and misread his kindness ; Cecilia exposed herself to criticism from the prudent.

PERSUASION

(WRITTEN 1815, 1816 : PUBLISHED, POSTHUMOUSLY, 1818)

ALTHOUGH the basis of this story repeats from *Pride and Prejudice* the surprising superiority, in this case of *one* sister, Anne Elliot, to the rest of her family, everything here depends upon a tender and deep emotion, never before attempted by Jane Austen. This most womanly heroine had given her heart, before the story opens, to the gallant and somewhat impetuous Captain Frederick Wentworth. But her lack of self-confidence and alarm at injuring his career, unfortunately encouraged by the prudence of a worthy matron and true friend, Lady Russell, almost a mother to Anne, had persuaded her of the unwisdom of long engagements, and led to his leaving her in anger, approaching contempt. His promotion, in fact, proved rapid ; and wisdom had been convicted unwise.

The story is wholly concerned with their meeting again ; and the gradual development from his indifference, to a deeper and more understanding love : won by her constancy and faith.

At first Wentworth appears, like Henry Crawford, thoughtlessly flirting with two sisters at once. Mary, second daughter of the childishly vain Sir Walter Elliot, had married Charles Musgrove of Uppercross ; whose sisters Henrietta and Louisa are, at first, both equally flattered by Wentworth's attentions ; but Henrietta quickly resumes her loyalty to a convenient cousin curate, and the Captain finding himself generally assigned to the high-spirited and, otherwise disengaged, Louisa, feels in honour bound to propose. Anne's influence was felt, but he had no suspicions of her feelings. At this point, Fate luckily intervenes to save the hero from actually committing himself, giving Louisa to James Benwick : clearing the field for Anne.

Understanding is reached at last, in a scene of intense, though quiet, emotion ; which, while perfectly dramatic, reveals Jane Austen's deepest convictions upon the true nature of woman.

The worldly atmosphere of *Mansfield Park* is here revived in the person of William Elliot, Sir Walter's heir, always intended for the cold-hearted eldest daughter ; but vastly preferring Anne. Here, again, intellectual sympathy, genuine taste, and accomplished manners are seen to strongly attract ; but, like Fanny Price, Anne is governed by principle and her instincts distrust the polish of his veneer. He has, in fact, been dissipated in youth ; his present virtues are but calculated ambition ; and experience has taught her to choose the risks of frank, openminded, confidence in one's own feelings and hopes : the love of youth learned in maturity.

There are many persons and events in this subdued tale, none conspicuously comic as in the earlier novels ; but drawn with exquisite humour in swift, telling phrase. It is entirely studied from life, with no borrowed character or scene ; the last, most perfect and perfectly constructed, expression of the author's art.

It is a remarkable fact, characteristic of Jane Austen's dislike for sensational emotion, that no death occurs, of characters actually present, in any of these novels. The influence of death, indeed, is strongly felt by Frank Churchill ; but this is the only occasion in which death occurs during the story. Memories of Dick Musgrove, Mrs Tilney, and others are felt in different ways.

Apart from the Church, and the Navy—both represented in her own family—the only professionals introduced are John Knightley (who was clearly a lawyer); Dr Parry and a few doctors, casually named; the schoolmistress, Mrs Goddard; Jane Fairfax and Mrs Weston, governesses; and a lady companion. We meet also a few Army men.

Naval characters are honourably distinguished in *Persuasion* by Admiral Croft, Captain Harville, James Benwick, and the hero himself; while the villains of *Mansfield Park* owe their lack of principle to an Admiral " of vicious conduct "; as Fanny's happiness largely depends on Midshipman William, and her most acute miseries were due to a Lieutenant of the Marines.

Several families have made their money in trade : Mr Gardiner lives over his shop.

The County is, naturally, represented in these tales; but the ' ordinary ' characters all live in " the village "; or in houses " with a separate lawn and shrubberies and name "— really " belonging " thereto; except when visiting Bath, Portsmouth, or Lyme Regis; occasional scenes in London are ' reported,' not described; save for the miserable weeks of the Dashwoods' visit to Mrs Jennings, including a few minutes in Bond Street. The peculiar social relations, and habits, produced by intimate friends and relations living on one estate, in " a cottage " or at " the Great House," as the Austens lived in Chawton, were anticipated in *Sense and Sensibility* and reproduced in *Persuasion*. The similar case of the Rev. Edward Ferrars at Barton, with a brother-in-law for neighbour and patron, gave more satisfaction, I suspect, than the ' Peeps at Rosings,' so much enjoyed by Collins.

LIFE AND FAMILY

The Rev. George Austen, 1731-1805 ; rector of Steventon, Hants.

Mrs Austen (Cassandra Leigh), 1739-1827 ; niece of Theophilus Leigh, Master of Balliol.

Their children :—

Rev. James, 1765-1819 : married (1) Anne Matthew ; (2) Mary Lloyd. A cultured scholar, largely responsible for forming Jane's literary tastes. His father's curate and successor.

Edward, 1767-1852 ; took the name of Knight, with the estates left him by his father's cousin and patron, Thomas Knight : married Elizabeth Bridges. A cheerful and kindly man of affairs.

Henry, 1771-1850 : married (1) Eliza de Feuillade, widow-daughter of his aunt, Mrs Hancock ; (2) Eleanor Jackson. Took orders in 1816. Jane's favourite brother. The handsomest and most brilliant of them all ; with a sunny temperament, but inclined to " tall talk," when serious.

Cassandra, 1773-1845. Engaged, about 1795, to Thomas Fowle, who died, 1797, in the West Indies.

Sir Francis (Frank), 1774-1865. Admiral of the Fleet : married (1) Mary Gibson ; (2) Martha Lloyd, sister to Mrs James. A grave and industrious gentleman ; the most, publicly, distinguished member of the family.

Jane, 1775–1817.

Charles, 1779–1852 : married (1) Fanny Palmer ; (2) Harriet
Palmer. The sisters' " own particular little brother,"
whose " death was a great grief to all the Fleet."

James had two children, Edward twelve ; Frank and Charles,
each a number indicated in the family tree by the word " etc."

Apart from occasional visits to friends or relatives and the
brief schooldays at Reading, Jane's whole childhood and youth
were spent in the country Rectory of Steventon. When the
Rector had given up his living to James, the family migrated
to Bath, in 1801 ; where Mr Leigh Perrot (Mrs Austen's
brother) was then living, and where the Rev. George died in
1805. During these years, tours, or visits, were made to Lyme
Regis, Sidmouth, Dawlish, and Teignmouth.

After their father's death, and visits to Clifton, Addlestrop,
and Stoneleigh, the widow and daughters settled in Southampton
from the winter of 1806–07 until 1809 ; joined by Martha
Lloyd, later Mrs Frank.

The second, and last, home was found, July 1809, in a cottage
at Chawton, on Edward's estate, near the " Great House,"
often occupied by the Knights, or lent to one of his naval
brothers. There were visits to Henry, now in London ; or
" a morning's drive " would easily carry them to Steventon and
the Rev. James.

Jane only left Chawton for Winchester in May 1817, just two
months before she was buried in the Cathedral.

INDEX

PRINTED IN GREAT BRITAIN BY NEILL AND CO., LTD., EDINBURGH.